WOMEN'S SUPERIORITY

WOMEN'S SUPERIORITY

....Through Quran

Dr Zubeda Baig

GYAN

ISBN : 978-81-2121-311-0
Price : ₹ 590

First Published 2016

Published by

Gyan Publishing House
5, Ansari Road, Darya Ganj
New Delhi-110002
Mob : 9811692060
E-mail: books@gyanbooks.com
Website : www.gyanbooks.com

Printed at : G. Print Process, Delhi

Cataloging in Publication Data—DK
Courtesy: D.K. Agencies (P) Ltd. <docinfo@dkagencies.com>

Baig, Zubeda, author.
Women's superiority : ....through Quran / Dr. Zubeda Baig.
pages cm
Includes bibliographical references.
ISBN 9788121213110

1. Women—Psychology. 2. Sex discrimination against women. 3. Women's rights. 4. Muslim women—Social conditions. 5. Women—Religious aspects—Islam. 6. Women in the Qur¼an. I. Title.

HQ1206.B35 2015 DDC 155.333 23

DEDICATION

This book is dedicated to all the Women and Girls of the world

Contents

Acknowledgements 11

Preface 13

1. **Introduction** 15
Why Men are Bad?
Why women are not doing anything? All... are not enough; even oprah chooses obama and not Hillary for President?

2. **The Superiority of Women** 29
Myth about women and their real superiority...
Women are not standing up for other women and their daughters.

3. **World Religion** 65
World religion speaks the same language, to put women down. They all say to put women in their place.
Most men want to put women in their place... so they are denied for any rights – political, economical, social, religious or educational.

4. **Women's Rights and Superiority in Sixth Century** 77
What happened to women's rights that Qur'an gave in Sixth century?

Qur'an Vs Hadees – when mullas talk they think they know but it is bad interpretation by men.

5. **Conclusion** **125**
New rules and ideas about Human Rights gone
Education for every one... New thinking and interpretation for and by women.

Bibliography 163
Index 173

Foreword

Everybody is looking for gender equality but my approach is different, I see the superiority of women. Buddha said, "Enlightment give extra radiance and peaceful presence." He said, “I am awake” and I want all women to awaken to Buddha's enlightenment. For women to be awakened to great power, wisdom and universal compassion. I want my readers to be compassionate and wise. I want to spread the truth of Quranic teachings and not the teaching of men. Women should be as powerful as Allah wants them to be.

Acknowledgements

I would firstly thank Amina Wadud, an American Muslim, who is an Arabic and Quranic scholar. For the first time, here is an interpreter who is wholly women oriented and free from male influence in her interpretations from beginning to end. When she talks about the Quran with reference to women, though she never used the word "superiority", I can find women superiority in Quran as she has interpreted it. She is my *'guru'*. I want to be like her. Thank you Amina Wadud for your interpretation is hundred per cent for women.

Next, I would like to thank Barbara Freyyer, an American. Her book is another Godsend for me. She is a Christian and Arabic Scholar in America and she is doing her interpretation free of men's influence. I salute her bravery for supporting Muslim women.

I also wish to thank Kaukab Siddique for his interpretation is completely for women. He is talking entirely on gender equality and proving it too. Thank you.

Lastly, I would like to thank the late Asghar Ali Engineer who had been working tirelessly for the Muslim women's gender equality. His forty some books are all for Quranic gender equality. In all his books he supported gender equality in Quran. He was against gender wars, pulling women down, four marriages and he did not support the Sahriah either.

He worked tirelessly for the Muslim women and community. He had been awarded several awards nationally and internationally, including the Right Livelihood award, also known as alternate Noble Prize. He had received honorary doctorates from three Universities. He had travelled throughout the world for lectures in different Universities. He was also my *'guru'*. My *'salam'* and my love to him!

Dr Zubeda Baig

Preface

In the time of the Prophet, one of his daughters was the keeper of the Quran. She maintained its safety and because of her guardianship we are allowed to read the original words of Allah 1400 years later. After her, another woman was in charge of the Holy Book. Only women can be responsible for the safe-keeping of the Quran and Islam. Women need to again become scholars of Arabic so they can translate the original words, and not rely on the translation of men. (Unfortunately I am not a scholar in Arabic and have had to rely on other female scholars.) I hope that mothers will help their daughters to be the future of Islam and the safe keepers of the Quran.

1

Introduction

Why Men are Bad?

Why women are not doing anything about women's position? All are not doing enough; even Oprah chooses Obama and not Hillary for President...

Women of the world come and stand beside me. Since my childhood I was thinking, why I and only I am the one who has the self-confidence and I'm not afraid, of criticising men for their past and present behaviour? Why we women have to feel so low so that you men can feel strong?

Women are considered as devil. Reason is that it is believed all evil and bad things happen in the world because of women. Why society is serving only men? All power, money, education, land, including women is all for men, to do all cruel things like abuse, torture and murder.

Now here is a new book proven for women's betterment. Women have been mostly ignored by men and religion. Religions have given people the idea that women are on earth to serve men. They have forgotten that everything in this world belongs to all humans, not just men. All over the world, women are working hard to prove that without their help nations will not succeed. Men must learn new realities about women, and new scientific facts about women. Societies all over the world have to learn new norms pertaining to women. After this, there will be gender superiority without any old biases. When this world is not "a man's world" but becomes a "human world" and a safe place for women, there will be gender superiority for women. When harassment is eradicated, a true world of gender superiority can exist. When the birth of a daughter makes her parents happy, then there is superiority.[1]

When Nehru said, *"I say it by way of emphasising the importance of mothers and daughters and sisters of a nation. One of the truest measures of a nation's advancement is the state of its women. Out of women comes the new generation and it is from their lips and laps that they begin to learn"*. He said in all other places that *"in rural India men and women worked equally in fields and it is only when we get to the middle that class distinction arises"*.[2]

In the middle class, the distribution of work between the men and women is well defined. While the men are involved in the decision-making and commanding position, the women are expected to play a subservient role of the implementer who ideally does not question any decision or command of the male member. The total responsibility of child rearing is the mother's job. The Committee on the Status of Women in India's report, "Today's Equality", was a gender specific report which influenced much of the women's movement in India. The report concluded that the typical family is the reason for women's oppression. Women need to know their position and their rights and the government wants to help women.

If one analyses a woman's life, she is the one who protects the family from all odds and she is the one who creates life by giving birth to a child in the family. A woman in her own life span can care for up to three generations. Despite such an important role in a family she is least respected by the family and society. That is why women have to be awakened so that they may become aware of their rights. Education can provide them with this awareness. They have to develop a great will to change the society. A woman is in her own person, an individual, too. To give women power, they have to work together as groups thinking for each other's issues and solving problems together.[3]

The Indian society needs laws to change its attitude towards women. Indian social norms are anti-women, so society has to be changed through new ideology by the help of government power. The Indian family keeps women dependent and powerless. When women get equal rights in marriage, land property and equal shares of a nation's productive resources, then only they will be economically and socially superior.[4]

To discuss disabilities and inequalities imposed on women, one needs to learn about the Indian society. The entire relationship of gender roles must change to give and in order to bring gender superiority. The question arises: why women are living like this with minimum dignity? To get the answer, we need to analyse: (a) the myth about men's superiority and women's disabilities, and (b) our social evils like dowry, *Sati*, female infanticide.[5]

After independence, Indian society has gone through many social movements to change the current social system. These movements made women aware and the constitutional provisions have made her more powerful. Women suffer miserably throughout their lives, however, it is insisted that women are like goddesses in India. After realising their position women are now fighting for basic rights and some dignity in a male-dominated society.

In a controversial statement the Chief Justice of the Supreme Court said once in his public speech in November 1990, that he wants every woman to go back home, let go of their jobs and make their homes a haven. Even after hearing this speech, there were small protests by a group of few angry women, but it was no big deal for the society.[6]

The Male's False Superiority Attitude

To understand why women are in this subordinate position in society it is important to know a man's attitude. Actually, man has a very convincing image of women according to which women are inferior due to their biological differences. Though a woman has the capacity to reproduce a child, they are denied an important role in the public or commercial sphere. History is written by men who do not tell the roles that women played in history. Now women issues are being explored in new light. Researchers are going on studying about women's body and mind. Due to these scientific findings it has now become obvious that women are not only as good and competent as men, but superior to them. Probably, that's why men kept women from gaining this knowledge.

Society needs to understand why all male philosophers wrote against women, right from Aristotle, Locke, and Hobbs, etc. all had one belief that women are weak, morally bad and should be controlled. Now women are proving that they are not weak or stupid as men think, but they are fully capable of handling jobs and families by themselves. Women have to learn new roles for themselves in every walk of life.[7]

Matriarchal Society in India

The Indian society is not totally a patriarchal setup. In certain regions of India, women enjoy more powerful position due to the matrilineal society. In one of the interesting researches, M. French, in her observations of India, found that even though, South Indian communities have matrilineal family their communities are strong. South Tamil Nadu, South Karnataka and Kerala most of all still have well established matrilineal families. Even Muslims have matrilineal households. The most well-known matrilineal households are of the *Nayars,* which is a high caste and landlord women community. Their property passes to their daughters. Men only visit their wives at night and go back to live with their mothers or grandmothers. Women can marry as many men as she wants (polyandry). The only rule is that the husband should belong to her caste or to the higher caste. In contrast to traditional Indian culture, older women hold authority in the house. No women in the community are abused because of widowhood. Girl's marriages are arranged as social and economic gain in alliance with other families, so girls are brought in not taken out. A woman can divorce her husband by simply putting her husband's belongings outside the house. The British outlawed these marriages, but they are still prevalent in South Indian Society. The matriarchal practice is also well established in the North Eastern tribal community. The women in these tribes have a strong position than the men due to ownership of property and the children are known by their mother's name.[8]

Now, let's discuss Muslim Women in India. They cannot go to the mosques and pray. They can pray at any place, even in churches, mandirs, roads, any rooms, planes, cars, or trains but not in mosques and they are not complaining. They cannot talk about early age and other women. Muslim women had some wonderful rights before any other women, but now why are they far behind other women?[9]

It is true that the data collected for Muslim women studies are not perfect or complete and lack the information belonging to all groups of women, their economic status, and urban and rural differences in education and society. But one thing is clear; Muslims are not leading women for women's rights like they were leading in sixth century. They lack education, are deprived socially and legally, and in a desperate need of women leaders amongst themselves, they have to cut their shackles of old customs like their Hindu sisters and stand together to demand their own rights, legally and religiously.[10]

Problems of rural women are much more serious and different than urban women with education and middle class and rich status. These women who worry about inheritance and husband's money and property, want their fair share, not what men want to give them.

Western authorities and research scholars have biased opinions of Islam. They are thinking that Islam treats women as slaves, but the reality of the Qur'an is totally different. Indian Muslim women are not aware of the real Qur'an; men did a good job to secure themselves. They try very hard till now to put women in their places, as soon as the Prophet closed his eyes. But now it is women's duty to go back to revolutionary spirit of Islam, free of any culture and free of any women hating men's personal hiding as Islamic rules, fooling the educated and uneducated people.[11]

Women want Gender Jihad for securing women's superiority. Let women have an awareness and an arising, as it is essential to start the momentum of setting women free from the shackles of so called religious sanctions.

Shariah Law which is considered the sole law of Islamic faith is not **Qur'anic law**. Some interpretations put together by the British are without women's rights, as in the 'Bible'. And now Muslims are dying to save what the British had **made law** just because Muslims do not want to lose their special identity in the constitution. They are exploiting and suppressing their women with practices of polygamy, and taking away their right to choose marriage partners and have property right to keep her last name after marriage, and adopting *Purdah* as *Burqah* essentially a culture and custom from Iran. Indian and other customs became Islam. Hindu women got their rights at least on paper with Hindu code, but Muslim women are still waiting for their rights even on paper. If Muslim women tried to be equal with men, they are declared 'non-Muslims' or enemy of Islam.[12]

Indu Singh is so right when she called this system the 'partiadate' where all the men get everything just because they are men not because they are worthy of it. This is the only way the system works. Women are not paid for their house job which makes them dependent because they are not employed, and now they are worthless in a materialistic society. They become cheap labour and are inferior and subordinate beings. At the time of divorces, Muslim women are deprived of all kinds of long time economic support, all in the name of religion. The question now arises, whose religion is this, Qur'anic or men? Taking care of each other, even so much, that rape has to be witnessed by "four men". Ridiculous! It is how men get together to deprive women of every dignity as a human being. Old Muslim scholars are impressed and derived their philosophy from Greek scholars. In the tenth or eleventh century, men believed that women were evil, stupid and worth being exploited, and be demanded full submission to men, who denied and ignored women's right to earn, share wealth and have her individuality as provided by the Qur'an. In spite of the revolutionary spirit of the Qur'an, men are still keeping women in the house, dependent on them, so they can have families and keep men in charge. Muslims learned old society's ways for the success of patriarchal system. The worst thing about all this is that uneducated women are doing everything to help men to suppress women as mothers and mothers-in-laws and sisters-in-law.[13]

Muslims are not secure about their religious identity in India. Bad feelings and communal infighting make Muslims' situation worse. Zamidari abolitions mean no land or income for most Muslims. They need their religious identity and social values. That is why they are thankful for **Shariah Law** without thinking that this is not **Qur'anic Law**. Because they don't have any Qur'anic understanding and no discussion on the matter, they make it un-Islamic to discuss the laws. The religious leaders insist that they get more power and control over all Muslims.

From Delhi University to Aligarh to Lucknow, girls are being educated not for jobs or for themselves but to be an educated wife, so their husband's status improves. This type of education is not helping women to discuss Shariah with men. Muslim women are segregates and have no education to change their situations through political power. They can demand new society and above all new women leaders to lead this new Muslim society, where they have a right to go to pray in a mosque, lead the gathering and pray, and need new interpretations of Qur'an without any men's influences like they are doing in Pakistan, every other Muslim and non-Muslim country.[14]

Religion has nothing to do with State policies in India. Muslim women have the same rights of education and employment in India. All laws for women welfare work is for them too. They have the same opportunities to do whatever they desire in constitutional rights. But the Muslim women are expected to observe *Purdah,* the rules of religion are all encompassing. They are expected to not only cover their head to toe, but no man, outside the family, are allowed to see them or talk to them, even when they are sick or need help. Their voice is heard only within the family. Women's life and their men's life are totally separate. Muslim women are not going to be seen or heard by anybody else, but family. Men are in the controlling position. Due to ignorance, illiteracy, most women follow men's control. If some women hate these traditions, then they are criticised. Muslim women are deprived of education and employment opportunities. If they have to have education, it is just meant for religious education, otherwise girls stay at home, while boys go to school. These practices are not in sync with the Qur'an which gave economic rights to women and to dress humbly and do whatever she wants to do. They are allowed to hold property and conduct their own business. Their right to job is equal to that of men.[15]

The Qur'an gave rights of earning their living to women, but men and their role in society take away that right from women, especially Muslim women. Now because of men's interpretation, woman is not being treated equally and has no economic independence and no equal rights with men.

Muslim women belong to all kind of different statuses and classes, and they live in different parts of the country. Their life is ruled by their economic status and their geographic status. Different parts of the country have different practices. North India is stricter with *Purdah,* but South India is not so strict, and more Muslim women have jobs and education. They make economic decisions in their houses. Non-*Purdah* means more involvement with rights of a normal life including education and employment and attitude towards life. With education they have a world of opportunity and understanding of equal rights in modern times and the Qur'an's new interpretation. Customs and traditions of Muslim women vary from culture to culture and region to region in India.[16]

As we know that South Indian Muslims are more modern and more educated, and they are taking care of their daughters as much as their sons. When they have good jobs, then they gain respect from society. It is evident from Tamil, Telugu, Malayali regional cultures. They want the same or better life for their daughters. When they are poor, then it is difficult to send their daughters to school and then the cycle of poverty repeats itself because of the lack of opportunity. It is the worst thing that happens to poor women. Muslim women as daughters, as sisters, as wives, as mothers and as grandmothers have rights to share property with men, but the Qur'anic share is gone and local customs prevail because they favour men. Women now have no holding over land or any kind of property and this way they lose respect and chances to live better and equal lives.[17]

If Muslim women can afford a better life, they can hope for a better future for their daughters where they are better educated, can live without *Purdah* and with a good job, they can do work for the betterment of the society and themselves and may become proud of their womanhood.[18]

Muslim community is a minority community. After Independence, Muslim community lost its place as a strong and rich community. People lost their land and livelihood, and most of them became poor and minority citizens of India. These positions make Muslim men too sensitive for their individual identity and they needed this blanket of separate family law for themselves. Now men are secured, but Muslim women lost their rights for the sake of community. If they want new interpretation, then they become Western women. Women suffer because they don't have real knowledge of the Qur'an.

Women who learn Arabic, learn and understand the Qur'an are needed to talk to men with their education and understanding of Qur'an. If Muslim men realise the real situation it will make a good community. If women get equal position with men as the Qur'an wants them to be, then Muslim community will regain the past glory.[19]

Education can give women more power and prestige among family members both men and women. It gives them an edge to sustain themselves in the society. Though the problems are immense, educated women are better treated. However, they encounter some general problems. For example, even at the high positions, women have problems of safety if they have to go out and work late at night. So women mobility is not easy, and this affects their promotion.[20]

A woman suffers too much when in place of her a man gets promotion, and she has to work under a man who is inferior to her in every way, education, experience, knowledge and intellect. It is really necessary for a woman not to sacrifice outside the home, and be ready to fight for her promotion, and telling everybody that she knows her rights and regulations of the job. Women have reservations in jobs, but not in promotions.

Educated women assert their economic independence, and they want to go out and compete in politics and in jobs equally with men. Women know that their lives are not for serving men or for raising children. They are becoming new role models for young girls. Girls are realising that they can be as successful as boys in schools, jobs and politics or in management, and they are better off when they have their own economics status. With status, they get respect from others, and have their own economic status. With status, they get respect from others, and self-respect is very important for today's woman. Men must learn to share household duties, children and be good to their wives and daughters. There would be a change in old traditions to accommodate new ones, like women are not helpless and weak, and education is important for both genders men have to know by now women have rights in family's money and property.

The origin of the English word, 'woman' indicates that the females' very right to social existence was determined in the light of the secondary relationship to the male for whom the world was originally formed. *"Woman"* is derived from the word, *'Wifman'* that is *wife-man*, the wife of the man. In the fourteenth century the 'f' was dropped and the word became *'wiman'* and later *'woman'*. Men consciously have desired to keep women in a secondary position to all. The rationalisations have offered for keeping her there has avoided the statement of their actual motivations because in most cases they have not consciously been aware of the nature of that motivation. Men must toil and women must spin, because if women stop spinning to start toiling, man's claim to creativity and indispensability as breadwinners is undermined and this he must resist.

Men have resisted the "intrusion" of women into their workaday world to the last ditch and many are still doing it.

Why? May it not be that such men feel that the working woman constitutes a threat to believe in themselves as the pillars of the society, the creation of civilisation?

However, when confronted with a challenge such as a woman holding a male-dominated position, the male often loses his balance. Rocking the boat is what it is. The best way therefore, to avoid such disturbances is to restrict women to the role of the helpless female who wouldn't know what to do with an oar or an engine if her life depended on it. Its man the boat and women and children first. And of course a certain number of men have to get into the boat otherwise the women wouldn't be able to manage.[21]

The Need to Read and Interpret the Qur'an from a Woman's Perspective

When I was doing research for my book, I read Amina Wadud Oman' book on women and after 15 years of research my dream came true. I found someone who thinks like me and is reading Qur'an like me and is biased as a woman that men were interpreting Qur'an for years and used words in their favour. For the first time, Amina not using the word superiority, but proving it she understands very well that every reader when reading Qur'an is unique, the understanding is unique too. I am trying to prove "Women Superiority" through Qur'an and her book is God sent. How women interpretation is different than man? I have my own interpretation for men and reading Qur'an through a woman's eyes.

No method of Qur'anic exegesis is fully objective. Each exegete makes some subjective choices. Some details of their interpretations reflect their subjective choices and not necessarily the intent of the text. Yet, often no distinction is made between text interpretations. I put interpretation of woman in the Qur'an into two categories – traditional and reactive.

The first category of the Qur'anic interpretation is the traditional interpretation. Traditional *tafsir* (exegetical works) give interpretation of the entire Qur'an whether from the modern or classical periods, with certain objectives in mind. Those objectives could be legal, esoteric, grammatical, rhetorical or historical.

The traditional *tafsirs* were exclusively written by males. This means, men and men's experiences were included and women and their experiences were either excluded or interpreted through the males' vision, perspective, desire or needs of women. In the final analysis the creation of the basic paradigms through which we examine and discuss the Qur'an and Qur'anic interpretation were generated without the participation and first hand representation of women. Their voicelessness during critical periods of development in Qur'anic interpretation has not gone unnoticed, but it has been mistakenly equated with voicelessness in the text itself.

The second category of Qur'anic interpretation concerned with the issue of modern women consists primarily of modern scholar's reaction to severe handicaps for women as an individual and as a member of society which have been attributed to the text. In this category there are many women and/or persons opposed to the Qur'anic message (or more precisely, to Islam), altogether. They use the poor status of women in Muslim societies as justification for their 'reactions'. These reactions have also failed to draw a distinction between the interpretation and text.[22]

The Voice of the Muslim Women

"Muslim Women speak for themselves. Please?"

The purpose of this book is to give evidence of and voice to the diversity of expressions that, constitutes contemporary Muslim women's scholarship and activism in the US. What makes this book unique and of critical importance in, understanding the current situation of Muslim women's subsidies in America can be understood by the genesis methodology and goals of this work. In summary, these women's writings can be seen as the product of the gradual but steady emergence of a movement among many perhaps a critical mass of Muslim women who insist that their religious self-identity (woman) not dismissed in fact it be affirmed in the amidst of their acknowledgement of and striving towards solving what they see as continue to face both women in Muslim and non-Muslim societies and communities around the world. This approval to Muslim women's scholarship and activism has been designated because it originates in the conviction that to look at woman's issues from within the Islamic women's perspective must include and indeed unite issues of theory and practice.

This means that any analysis or theory of women's nature role, rights or problems must include attention to the practical, immediate issues involved in actualising the Qur'anic mandate of social justice and concomitantly that any consideration of practical solution accompany.

I insist again that when I was doing research for my book, I read Amina Wadud Oman and women and after 15 years of research my dream came true. Someone who thinks like me and reading Qur'an like me biased as a woman, men were interpreting Qur'an for years and used words in their favour. For the first time Amina not using the word superiority, but proving it she understand very well that every reader when reading Qur'an is unique, the understanding is unique too. I am trying to prove "Women Superiority" through Qur'an and her book is God sent. How women interpretation is different than man? I want respect for every woman and reading Qur'an through a woman's eyes.[23]

2

The Superiority of Women

Myth about women and their real superiority...

Women are not standing up for other women and their daughters.

Women are just beginning to emerge from their long fettered period of subjection and the dictates and discrimination against them. It is of interest to recall as illustrative of and prevailing traditional attitudes toward women, that the entire article on "Woman" in the first edition of the *Encylopaedia Britannica,* published in 1771, consisted of six words "The female of man, See Homo".

Women have always been a convenient screen upon which men have projected their weaknesses and ambivalence for many men today. Attitudes towards women remain very much what they were during the nineteenth century.

Nineteenth century scientists and thinkers, with rare exceptions, were busily engaged in proving that women were inferior to men. Women, it was alleged had smaller brains than men, were much less intelligent, became more emotional and unstable in stressful situations, and were frigidly, weakly creatures. They couldn't be entrusted with handling money. They could be employed only at the most menial and routine tasks as servants, nannies or if they were adequately trained as governesses. The inferiority of women was a hoary headed ancient belief that everyone took for granted, a fact of nature beyond question. But this fact of nature was a prejudice, a myth.

What is a Prejudice? What is a Myth?

A prejudice is a prejudgment having no factual validity. A prejudgment or opinion held before the facts are known.

What then is a fact? A fact is a datum of experience which has been repeatedly tested and confirmed by independent investigators. The current best fit between reality and our method of confirming it. The greatest enemy of truth is not error but prejudice. It is the nature of myth to elaborate, but never to prove.

Since most people who have been to school or college have been taught what to think rather than how to think, they are consequently at the mercy of any juggler who chooses to reinforce their prejudices or create new ones for them to believe.

A myth is usually a traditional belief of unproven reality which serves to explain some phenomenon of nature, creation, humankind and supernatural, religion, persons, social conditions and the likes. Myths are often expedient fictions.

What then are the functions of myth? Myths perform the double function of serving as models of and models for cultural attitudes and behaviour. In this way they reflect the beliefs of and provide sanction for the actions of society, while at the same time furnishing the forms upon which belief and conduct are modelled.

Myths act as a force of daily life and of history. Racism is such a myth. In many cases to many religions myth are not accountable to reality.

Myths tend to become "realities". Such realities are often more to their believers than the truth which would show them to be unreal.

Shattering the Myth

It took World War I to create a dent in the myth of women's inferiority to begin the disintegration of some entrenched beliefs concerning female employability. Women for the first time were enlisted to replace men in occupations that were formerly the exclusively male preserves. Women became truck drivers, farm to factory workers, labourers, supervisors, train engineers, ticket collectors, executive officers, armed services. The truth was out; women can do as well as men in most of the fields that had been closed to them for their supposedly natural incapacities.

Forty five years after WW I, women fully achieved their heaven. Meanwhile, sadly they also were taken to smoking, drinking and dancing in mushrooming dance floors. Somehow, the "new woman" not only managed to survive but also to prosper.

Most countries today are delinquent in attending to the rights of the women; all the rights to which human beings by virtue of humanity should be entitled. When the U.N. Charter was signed, only 36 countries in the whole world accorded women full political rights.

In US, the only right guaranteed to women is the right to vote and this was by the nineteenth Amendment to the Constitution, passed in 1919 largely through the work of Susan B. Anthony. Yet of all other rights, such as equal protection under the law, the right to jury service, the right to control and to enter any business or profession, the right not to be deprived of one's property without due process of law, the right to choose unrestrictedly the hours of work, the right to custody of children to divorce, or to freedom of speech, more is constitutionally guaranteed to women. A proposed Equal Rights Amendment (ERA) to the constitution has on several occasions, been an election year promise. In 1948, a Senate Judiciary Sub-committee recommended by a vote of seven to one that the amendment, "do pass" but no further action was taken. In 1972, the amendment was passed but Congress wanted the states for ratification, but failed to secure approval by the necessary minimum of thirty right states within ten years required for enactment.

What then is the Solution?

The solution lies in the re-evaluation of our values in a complete re-organisation of what today passes for education, but represents nothing more than instruction, a very different thing. Instruction is really just training in techniques and skills, the three R's. Such training is, of course, indispensably necessary, but it is only a limited part of what should be understood by *education*. The very word is derived from the Latin *educate,* meaning to nourish and to cause to grow. What is it that I should nourish and cause to grow? It is the basic behavioural needs of the child, the needs for growth and development as a physically and mentally healthy person, a whole person, one who is able to love, work, play and think soundly. These are the four great chords of Mental Health - that is what education should be about.

It is evident that because we have not understood the true meaning of education, that women have been suppressed in society.

Women's Place in Society

Women's place is considered in the home and the men's place in outside the house. However, a change is occurring. Women have entered the outside houses and are seated as members of a board of directors.

In September of 1953, the Eighth Assembly of the UN elected its first woman President Vijaya Laxmi Pandit of India. In 1960, Sirimavo Bandaranaika became Prime Minister of Sri Lanka (formerly Ceylon) the first woman in the world to hold such an office. In January 1966, Indira Gandhi was sworn in as Prime Minister of India. In March 1969, Golda Meir was elected Prime Minister of Israel. In 1970, Maria De

Lourdes Pintassilgo was appointed Prime Minister of Portugal. Margaret Thatcher was elected Prime Minister of the United Kingdom in 1979 and hold office until 1990, eleven and a half years longer than any previous Prime Minister in the twentieth century. In 1980, Lidia Gueiler Tejada was chosen by the congress of Bolivia to be the President of that country. In the same year Milka Planinc became Prime Minister of Yugoslavia. Mary Eugenia Charles became Prime Minister of Dominica. In 1981, Gro Harlem Brundtland a physician became the first woman Prime Minister of Norway. In 1988, Benazir Bhutto was elected Prime Minister of Pakistan. In 1989, Kazimiera Prunskiene was elected Prime Minister of Lithuania. In March 1990, Earthal Pascal – Trouillot, former attorney general, was sworn in as interim President of Haiti and in April 1990, Violeta Barrios de Chamorro was elected President of Nicaragua. In November 1990, Mary Robinson was the first woman elected President of Ireland. In May 1991, Edith Cresson became Prime Minister of France. It is beginning a very small one never the less.

Queen Elizabeth I of England been a heroin of English speaking world for five centuries and Queen Elizabeth of England is today of the most popular figures of the English speaking world. Queen Beatrice of the Netherlands is equally popular as was her mother Queen Juliana and grandmother Queen Wilhelmina. Queen Jadwiga (1373 - 99) of Poland, is remembered as one of the greatest rulers and one of the truly inspired peacemakers of history.

Queen Elizabeth 1 and Queen Victoria rank among the most notable English Monarchs and both their reigns coincided with a rise in prestige and prosperity such as England had never before experienced.[1]

The goddesses centered art with its striking absence of images of warfare and male domination reflect a social order in which women as heads of law or queens, priestesses played a central role.

The striking fewness of male figurine and the overwhelming member of female ones suggest the powerful role of women played in prehistoric societies. Finally, it seems clear that such societies were characterised by peace, co-operation and freedom, without war or conflict of any kind.

Significance of the fact then is that women have been made to feel like handicaps for their life giving role.

In many of the tribes (Australian Aboriginals) peoples is common belief that it is the spirit child that has entered the male first as he dreamed it. Should he desire a child, he tells his wife what has happened and the child is then transferred to her. Even then she is merely regarded as the incubator of the child planted in her by the male.

The idea is clearly expressed by the Greek dramatist Aeschylus (525–456 B.C.) in his play, *Ecemenides* in which Athene the daughter of Zeus who sprang from his head is made to say "The parent that which is called her child is not really the mother of it. She is but the nurse of the newly conceived foetus. It is the male who is the author of its being, which she as a stranger (that is to say no blood relation) preserves the young plant.

The very terms we use when we speak of male and female roles in reproduction, like the terms 'male' and 'female' themselves, and also men and women make woman subservient and addendum to men and reflect the ignorance and prejudice that have characterised the dominant male attitudes. The male fertilises, fecundates or impregnates the female. The truth, however is quite otherwise the process of reproduction is not one sided. Its antecedent condition is the fusion of two cells, the female ovum and the male sperm. It is not that an ovum is rendered foetile by the sperm, but that ovum and sperm contribute to the initiation of those further processes that result in an embryo's development. Furthermore, all embryos up to the end of the sixth week are female. The ovum has a volume approximately 85 thousand times greater than that of the sperm because it carries the nutriment necessary for the development of the early conceptions.

Hysterectomies were performed in 1975, resulting in 1,700 deaths. It was estimated that surgery was unnecessary in 22 per cent cases, resulting in 374 avoidable deaths. Can it be that in some cases the unconscious motivations for such operations differ from those consciously alleged? For further information on unnecessary surgical interventions the reader should refer to Dr Diana Scully's important book, *Men who Control Women's Health.*

Only among humans have male succeeded in stepping between a woman and a meal, in wresting control of the resources that she needs to feed herself and her children. Only among humans is the idea even floated that a male should support a female and that female is, in fact, in capable of supporting herself and her offspring and that is a perfectly reasonable act of quid protocol to expect a man to feed his family and a woman to be unerringly faithful to give the man paternity assurance and to make his investment worthwhile.

"I am convinced that male control over productive resources needed by women to reproduce lies at the heart of the transformation from male-dominated, male philopatric primate societies to fully fledged patriarchy".

The standard model of human evolution, the long dependency of children necessitated increased paternal investment in a child's welfare, and woman wanted, needed, demanded male help in meaning children, males could provide that help by hunting and bring home meat, which is rich in calories and appeals to the hominid tongue so smartly. By this scenario and origin of marriage and human pair bond and of female dependency on males are ancient 100s and 1000s of years old from an inchoate eposes that evolutionary theorists refer to as an "environment of evolutionary adaptability", then we supposedly became us, genetically and pre-dispositional. And by this scenario a woman began seeking a man and signs of wealth and power and wherewithal to support her and her children. While a man began seeking in a woman a sign of fecundity, a youthful capacity to breed a large brood as well as a signs that such fecundity would be reserved for him and provided if he was to invest in her and her offspring, he didn't want to be investing in offspring that were not his.

Now the conventional model of man the hunter is under persuasive attack, called in question by Kristen Hawkes and many others, whose recent analyses of traditional foraging societies suggest that male hunting counts for very little in the daily sustenance of their families and that network of women gathers most of the calories to keep the kinfolk fed. The new work suggests that among ancestral humans, women still had strong degree of autonomy, as chimpanzee females do, as the females of all other primates do and that the "patriarchy" the "nuclear family" call it what you will, but it is the dependence of women and men for their butter and bread – is at least on a long and codified scale, a fairly recent event in human prehistory. The transformation may be one of the fruits of the agricultural revolution as a number of historians and evolutionary scientists have proposed.

"With the advent of intensive agricultural and animal husbandry, women, by and large, lost control over the fruits of their labours" Smuts has written. "Foraging and nomadic slash – and even horticulture requires vast areas of land and mobile females, making it more difficult for men to control women's resource base and to restrict women's movements. However, when women's labour is restricted to a relatively small plot of land as in intensive agriculture or in restricted primarily to the household compounds as in animal husbandry, it is easier for men to control both the resource base upon which women depend for subsistence and women's daily movements.[2]

Almost without exception women face better in a matrilocal system, in which they stay where they were born, are surrounded by their friends and relations to have their men folk move in than they do when they must have home to join their husband's domain. The Iroquois, for example, were a strongly matrilocal culture and the Iroquois had one of the most egalitarian cultures known to anthropology. But the more women came to be seen as resources to be bartered the less sense it made to oblige them by moving in their pitched tents.

Some biblical scholars have seen in Genesis a recapitulation of the struggle to replace matrilocality with patrilocality, a critical step in enabling the Hebrew tribe to exchange nomadism for stateism, centred on the rule of the patriarch. Early, in Genesis 2: 24, is the passage, *"Therefore shall a man leave his father and mother and shall cleave unto his wife", is a likely reference to a matrilocal system of wedlock.*[3]

Evolutionary Psychology

Lately, the idea has found new fodder and new fans through the explosive growth of a field known as evolutionary psychology. Evolutionary psychology professes to have discovered the fundamental modules of human nature most notably the essential nature of man and of a woman.

Evolutionary psychology likes to think of itself as new and truthful, but it is really just a subset of sociobiology. E. O. Wilson defined his field as "the systematic study of the biological basis of all social behaviour".

The cardinal premises of evolutionary psychology of interest to our discussions as follows:

1. Men are more promiscuous and less sexually reserved than women are.

2. Women are inherently more interested in a stable relationship than men are.

3. Women are naturally attracted to high status and men with resources.
4. Men are naturally attracted to youth and beauty.
5. Our core preferences were hammered out long ago. Hundreds and thousands of years ago in the legendary environment of evolutionary adaptation or EFA, also known as the ancestral environment, also known as the Stone Age, and they have not changed appreciably since then nor are they likely to change in the future.

Do women find older men innately attractive? Is it the men's alpha stature or could it be something less complimentary to the male. Something like the following – that the older man is appealing, not because he is powerful but because in his maturity he has lost some of the power and has become less marketable and desirable and potentially more grateful and gracious, more likely to make a younger woman feel that there is a balance of power and relationship?

The rude little calculation is simple:

He is male, I am female – advantage man

He is older, I am younger – advantage woman

By and same token a woman may place little value on a man's appearance because she values something else for more room to breathe.[4]

Women of Power

Ela Bhatt is also leader from India. Her parents were Brahmin and she received a superb education leading to a law degree in 1955. She joined the legal department of the Textile Labour Association (TLA), founded by Mahatma Gandhi, and soon became the leader of its women's wing. In 1972, when the textile mills of Ahmedabad, India's fifth largest city were failing the workers were laid off. Ela visited their neighbourhood and found that the women were supporting their family through vending and home based work like sewing and cigarette rolling. This work was low paying and exploitive. She became increasingly concerned when she realised there were state laws protecting Industrial workers, but not the thousands of self-employed women who worked to provide for their family.

With her income she organised them into the Self Employed Women's Association (SEWA) with herself as the General Secretary. She followed the example of Gandhi who believed an organisation of workers should cover all aspects of their lives as a holistic defense against oppressive laws of the State.

When Ela Bhatt received the Indira Gandhi Prize for Peace, Discrimination and Development in February 2013, she said:

"I have faith women in my experience as I have seen within India and in other countries; women are the key to rebuilding a community. Why? Focus on women you will find an ally who wants a stable community. She wants work for her family. You get a worker, a provider, a caretaker, an educator, a networker, a forger of bonds. I consider thousands of poor working women's participation and representation on integral part of the peace and development process. Women bring constructive, creative and sustainable solutions to the table. A woman, who tends a small plot of land, grows vegetables, weaves cloth, and provides for the family and the market while caring for the financial, social, educational and emotional needs of her family, is a multifunctional worker and the builder of a stable society.[5]

I have a voice so I speak. I was never hushed at my house and nor at my husband's home after marriage. Why all women are not allowed to express and speak their voice?"

"My message to all the young girls in our country is that sometimes your weakness can be your biggest strength and like the handicap in golf, your weakness can be your perceived weakness, work quietly on converting these into unwavering self confidence and decisiveness and then go out and conquer the world".

"My grandmother was a feisty, tough woman full of beans and boy oh boy she was a deliverer! She travelled all over the world, had five kids, lived her life with unstoppable enthusiasm and energy and had complete conviction that her faith would see her and her family through life. She was my hero and she left a lasting impression on my life. That is what I want you all to remember, leave a lasting impression on your family".[6]

Originally published in 1984, *'Goddesses in Every Woman'*, presented a new psychology of women based on the goddesses of ancient Greece, whose names and mythologies have endured for more than 3000 years. It became a bestseller and there was never out of print classic like a woman with good bone structure, seemingly ageless.

'Goddesses in Every Woman', brought together what I knew as a psychiatrist and analyst, and as a woman in an evangelist of feminism. I saw uniquely female way of being and behaving that were rewarded or rejected by patriarchal judgments. I also recognised underlying personality patterns that determined how an individual woman responded to unwanted events and mythology and there I found remarkable parallels that transformed my thinking. In myths about the Greek goddesses, every goddess has different qualities and varies and as a whole they include the full panorama of human attributes including attributes such as competitiveness and intelligence.[7]

It is an open question whether the real mainstay and support of the family in the psychological if not entirely in the material sense has not always been the wife and husband nor was she anywhere nearly as knowledgeable about so many of the things her husband had experienced, furthermore he was bigger and stronger than she. The children were even more inferior to their father than was their mother and boys of course, were superior to girls. To this day, most parents in the western world hope that train first born will be a boy. In societies that practiced infanticide, girls were invariably the principle victims. Growing up in such male-dominated societies as would be difficult to avoid the conclusion that males were superiors to females.

"Miss. S. Hadfield", in her little known book, ***"Letters on the Importance of the Female Sex, with Observations on their Manners and Education"***, published in 1803, called upon women everywhere to look beyond the traditional role expected of them by now. In her preface, she wrote, *"Men have, indeed, too long thought it an advantage to consign the fair sex to ignorance, that by a monopoly of knowledge their superiority might be supported"*.

In male supremacist cultures, women were never given equal opportunities with more opportunities for the development of their intelligence and were severely restricted by what was traditionally considered permissible to woman.[8]

The myth of female inferiority is so old like the fact that earth was flat. After all it was obvious because it was believed that the sun rose and set on the earth. Men are considered around 10 per cent bigger than women; therefore from a biological point of view confer greater survival benefit upon him?

Lesser size and muscular power of the female confer lesser survival benefits upon her. On the contrary the facts prove that the biological advantages are with the female.

The performance of the shorter, slighter, and weaker female suggests that the best woman can do as well as the best men and often even better. Ever since Gertrude Edeera of the United States, on August 6, 1926 swam the English Channel in fourteen hours 31 minutes, two hours faster than any man or woman had ever done before. There have been striking performances given by women, which testify to their remarkable physical skills and staying power.

On October 12, 1955, Florence Chadwick of the US crossed the Channel from England to France, the more difficult route in 13 hours and 10 minutes. On August 17, 1974, she made the same crossing in 12 hours and 22 minutes. The race from France to England in August 1957 in which both men and women competed was won by a woman swimmer, Greta Anderson of Denmark in 13 hours and 53 minutes. In September 1967, Linda Mc Gill, a 21 years old Australian broke the women's record by swimming the channel in nine hours, 39 minutes missing the men's mark by only 24 minutes. In September 1971, Connie Ebelaar, a 22 years old Dutch swimming instructor swam the English Channel from England to France in 10 hours 40 minutes which was 20 minutes away from equaling the men's record for the 21 mile swim. Wendy Brooke of the US in September 1976 swam the Channel from France to England in 8 hours and 56 minutes the fastest time for anyone, male or female. More astonishing is the performance of Peggy Lee Dean of the US who in July 1978 set a record for the fastest Channel crossing from England to France for male and female in 7 hours and 40 minutes. Finally without adding any of the other Channel records achieved by the women then stands the unique accomplishments of Diana Nyad of the US, who in 1975 became the first person to swim non-stop the 32 miles across Lake Ontario.

Among all the women's physical superiority, women's body fat is much more than man, which is better insulated against cold than man. 25 per cent of body weight is fat in females compared with 14 per cent in males.

Women's narrower shoulder offers less resistance through the water. Women are also capable of caller are extra reserves of energy unavailable to men. Women are able to draw upon their fat reserve.

Women are able to deal with heat better than men, because women's greater numbers of sweat glands are distributed more uniformly over their bodies. Also blood supply to skin is more efficient so more blood is distributed to the surface to be cooled. The male sweats sooner, but the female sweats physiologically more efficiently. Women are also better equipped to deal with cold.

Another enduring race where not many have entered is the sled racing, which is run under the world's worst weather conditions on the 11,000 mile Alaska trail from Anchorage to Nome. In March 1990, Susan Bulcher won her fourth consecutive Alaskan race in record time. The terrain and weather presents a grueling challenge requiring great stamina cooking of meals for oneself and the dogs caring for their injuries little or no sleep and strength of character.

Physical force becomes most only a valued trait but also a sanctioned form of behaviour.

It is permissible to beat up ones wife and children in so many societies without even being questioned about it socially conferred superiority not biological once boys generally fight girls do not.

Let us apply another test: In life, the rigours of life, is well borne by whom, the male or the female? It is the female. Women endure all devitalising, exposure, fatigue, shock, illness and the likes. Isn't women supposed to be the weaker vessel? Weakness is a misleading word that has in this connection, confused people.

The fact is that the women are constitutionally much stronger than the male, have greater stamina and lives longer. Female possesses an immunological system that is more efficient and powerful than that of male this providing / affording greater immunity against infection and endowing her with a faster recovery rate. Compared to male, he burns himself out more rapidly and hence dies at an earlier age.

The general widespread belief that a larger or heavier brain constitutes a criterion of higher mental facilities is understandable enough, but it happens to be false.

For example, the Neanderthals had an average brain volume of 1,550 cubic centimeters, while the pre-historic humans of modern type, of South Africa had an average brain volume of 1,660 cubic centimeters compared with the modern human having an average of about 1,400 cubic centimeters.

Scientific investigations fairly numerous, say the brain size has no relation with intelligence. The biggest human brain on record was that of an idiot and one of the smallest was that of the French writer Anatole France. The idiot's brain weighed 2,850 grams and the brain of Anatole France weighed only 1,100 grams.

During the last century and the early parts of the twentieth century the great standby of men in arguing the inferiority of women was the lesser absolute size and weight of the female brain.

Among the Europeans the average weight of the male brains is about 1,385 grams and the female brain is 1,265 grams. The slight difference of four ounces between the male and female brain created a myth that men are more intelligent than women. Despite the evidence repeated again and again in edition after edition of Havelock Ellie's widely circulated book *"Man and Woman"* and in Amram Schefield's more recent "Women and Men" the myth seems to be strongly entrenched as ever.

The elephant and whale have a large brain size but no one has proved that they are as intelligent as the size of their brain is.

Eventually, in relation to body size the female brain is as large as in general as that of male. The complete facts have been available for more than a century, even since

Professor T.L.W. Bischoff, the great German anatomist, published his study on the brain weight of man. Das Hirnegewicht des Menschen, Bonn 1880, since then many other scientists have independently confirmed the findings of Bischoff, through many such to findings.

First everyone has female brain after couple of weeks the baby changes different brain better for human.

What are the Facts?

Bischoff and later others showed that the brain weight of the female in relation to male's brain weight is as 90:100, whereas her body weight is to the males only as 83:100. Now if I were to raise the female's body weight to the equivalent proportion of male namely, 100 units then one would have to add 17 units to the existing 90 for the female proportion of the brain to that of the male yielding a figure of 107 for a female as compared to 100 for the male. That is the proportion that most investigators have found when allowance has been made for body size. When one eliminates body fat from the weight of both sexes the difference in brain weight in favour of the female is further increased.

As stated previously we find that among Europeans that average brain weight of men is 1.385 grams three pounds and one ounce while that of a woman, is 1,265 grams. Now if the weight of the brain is considered in relation to the weight of the body, it will be found that women possess the relatively heavier brain. The average body weight of man is about 143 pounds; while that of women is 121 pounds then the average body weight of the male is about 22 pounds greater than that of the average female. Upon calculations it will be found that while man has one ounce of brain weight for every 45 ounces of body weight. Roughly speaking then the brain weight of woman constitutes about two per cent of the weight of the body, while the brain weight of a man is only one per cent of body weight. Of the brain the cortex is larger in females. French Neurosurgeon and physical anthropologist, Paul Broca, who was by no means an ardent feminist was the first to show that if one took the cerebral hemisphere to represent 1000 then the proportion of the frontal lobe to the hemisphere in the male is 427, whereas in the females it is 431.[9]

Most investigators appear to agree that intermediate region on the side of the brain known as the parietal area occupies a larger area in the male than in the female. The occipital lobe (the back part of the brain) most investigators find is equal size in both sexes. Woman has a better blood supply to the brain.

"Every woman has the leading role in her own unfolding life story. As a psychiatrist I have heard 100s of personal stories and I realise that there are mythic dimensions in every one. Some women come to see a psychiatrist when they are demoralised or not functioning, others when they wisely perceive that they are caught in a situation they need to understand and change. In either case it seems to me that women seek the help of a therapist in order to learn how to be better protagonists or heroines in their own life stories. To do so women need to make conscious choices that will shape their lives. Just as women used to be unconscious of the powerful effects that cultural stereotypes had on them, they may also be unconscious of powerful forces within them that influence what they do and how they feel".[10]

In any case, the status of the female is never in doubt. Whoever produces eggs is essential to the future, for eggs are reproductive cells whatever they must be.

Eggs of course also contribute their variability to the offspring, but eggs alone have the capacity, under certain conditions to develop readily into grown organisms, whereas sperms lack such a capacity altogether. In all species the mature organism is the developed egg, with extra touches added usually but not always, only when a sperm is involved.

Chromosomes which are neither X nor Y (22 in the haploid and 44 in the diploid state), are called 'autosomes'.

There are 22 pairs of them in the body cells but only 22 single ones in the sex cells. Each of the autosomes contains factors that tend toward the production of femaleness. The Y chromosome carries factors that are male – determining (Among the genes contained in the Y chromosomes is one responsible for the secretion of the masculinising hormone testosterone, from the gonads). Hence, when a Y carrying fuses with an ovum, the 22 pairs of autosomes carrying genes directed towards femaleness, are insufficiently powerful to reduce their influence, and the result is the development of a male. On the other hand, the combination of two X chromosomes, one from the mother, one from the father is sufficient to overcome the influence of any possible male factors in the autosomes and the result is female. The X chromosomes together have quite a pull to them and the explanation of the biological superiority of the females lies in the female having two X chromosomes while the male has only one. It is largely to the original X chromosomes deficiency of the male that almost all the troubles to which he falls heir may be tried and to the presence of two well appointed, well furnished X chromosomes that the female owes her biological superiority. As a consequence of the larger size of the X chromosome, the female's cells are about four per cent greater in chromosome volume than that of the males. As doctors J.H. Tipo and T.T. Puck who originally determined the difference in sex chromosome size in 1956 have remarked – "The female has a substantially richer genetic capacity than the male".[11]

Let us see how women's brain works. "In communal riots too men have been real culprits than women. In my 40 years of investigating and monitoring communal riots in India. I have not found a single instance in which any women plotted and executed riots, much less killed any Hindu or Muslim. It was only in Gujarat that a woman is alleged to have instigated men to kill human beings in Naroda Patia. I have found no other instance", said late Ali Asghar Engineer.

However, I have come across several instances in which women have saved lives of innocent people. These women are real inspiration for peace loving people. I would like to throw some light here on the rule of these women. Since I discovered while investigating riots and some, I read about in newspapers and subsequently met them and yet some we had the occasion to felicitate them on behalf of women for secularism, an organisation working for rights of women at grass roots.

This woman, a vegetable vendor, heard this and came out of her room with her sickle with which she used to cut her vegetables. She came downstairs and stood at the entrance challenging the mob to step forward to kill the Muslims, "I will cut the head of anyone coming forward with this sickle, and then you can kill me and walk over my dead body to kill the Muslims". None came forward and the mob of 500 dispersed. A Hindu mob came to set fire to the bus. They were mostly women and children going for the marriage.

Yadav was passing from there with her son. She saw that the bus will set fire killing 40 women and children. She looked around for something with which she could ward off the mob. She found an iron rod. Picked it up and charged with it. The mob ran away and she asked her son to drive the bus towards their hose. Fortunately, the driver had left the ignition key in the bus itself, enabling her son to drive the bus off to their compound this saving 40 lives, single handedly.

The Chief Minister Mulayam Singh Yadav himself met her and awarded her with one lakh of rupees for her courage. I also met her when I went to Aligarh for investigation. She said she was not sure whether she would be able to save their lives, but I considered it my duty to save innocent lives, especially women and children. They all would have been reduced to ashes. I am fortunate to have saved their lives.

Some of these women were Hasubai Buchare, Tekha Chanade, Vandana Gaikwad, Nisha Butade, all grass root workers. One of them in Icchalkaranji where we felicitated them on behalf of Women for Secularism in a convention held on 13th November 2009, I found them very courageous and though some of them were illiterate or had very little education, they spoke with great verve against those who organise communal violence to serve their political ends and vowed never to allow such violence in their village.

The communal violence in Kandhmal district wherein about 40 Christians were killed by some Hindu fanatics also saw many Hindu courageous women come forward to save the lives of Christian fellow villagers in 2008. Some of these women were Ranchi Pradhan, Sunechi Pradhan of Rudenia village, Satyabhama Nayak and Nibojni Pradhan, who showed exceptional courage in saving lives of many Christians or protect their houses. We felicitated all of them in a convention of All India Secular Forum (*Pradhan* is the title used by the village head).[12]

Women's Dignity

Firstly, when classical jurist were formulating laws the very social ethos was to subject women to make authority.

Secondly, there was no concept of rights of women as an individual entity and this certainly influenced Islamic jurists while making laws. They could not completely ignore the rights but did find ways to make women subordinate to men through arguments such as she is biologically different as a mother she has duties towards her children or by using a weak *ahadith* or the Qur'anic text through their own interpretation.

Thirdly, women in those days were economically totally dependent on man.

It was said that a 'Mehram man' must accompany his woman when he goes out. She was barred from going out alone. In those days social conditions was such that there was no security outside home. The women were considered weak and unable to defend themselves from sexual attack and molestation. Therefore, it was pronounced that a man must accompany her to protect her.[13]

The Female Brain

A graphic picture of a female brain

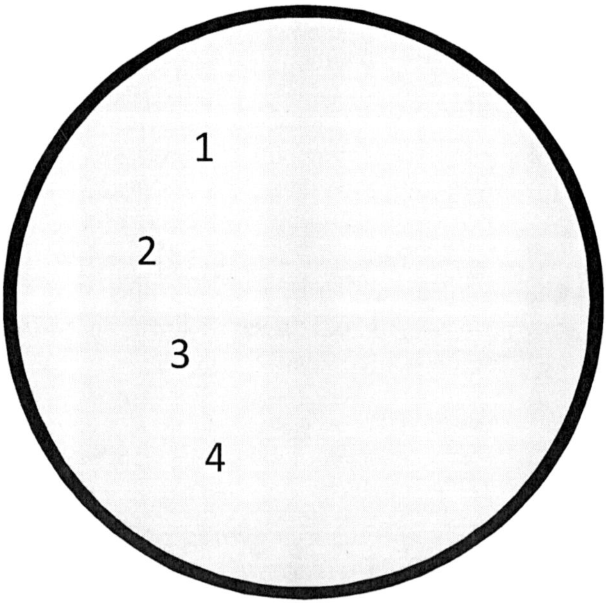

1. *Anterior Lingulate Cortex (ALC)*: Weighs options, makes decisions. It's the worry-work centre, and it is larger in women than in men.

2. *Prefrontal Cortex (PFC)*: The queen that rules the emotions and keeps them from going wild. It puts the brakes on the amygdale. Larger in women and matures faster in teen girls than in boys by one to two years.

3. *Insula:* The centre that processes gut feelings larger and more active in women.

4. *Hypothalamus*: The conductor of the hormonal symphony, and kicks the gonads into gear. Starts pumping earlier at puberty in females.

5. *Amygdala*: The wild beast within. It is the instinctual core that is tamed only be the PFC is larger than men.

6. *Pituitary Gland*: Produces hormones of fertility, milk production and nurturing behaviour. Helps turn on the mommy brain.

7. *Hippocampers*: The elephant that never forgets a fight, a romantic encounter or a tender moment – and won't let you forget it either, is larger and more active in women.

The cast of Neuro-hormone characters, (in other words, how hormones affect a woman's brain).

The ones your doctor knows about:

ESTROGEN – the queen, powerful, in control, all consuming, sometimes all business, sometimes and aggressive seductress, friend of dophamine, serotonin, oxytocic, acetylcholine and norepinephrine (the feel good brain chemicals).

PROGESTERONE – in the background but a powerful sister to estrogen, intermittently appears and sometimes is a storm.

TESTOSTERONE – fast assertive, focused, all consuming, masculine, forceful seduces, aggressive, unfeeling, has no time for cuddling.

The ones your doctor may not know about that also affect your brains:

OXYTOCIN – the fluffy purring kitty, cuddly, nurturing, earth, mother, the good witch Glinda in the *'Wizard of Oz'*, find pleasure in helping and serving, sister to vasopressin (the male socialising hormone), sister to estrogen, friend of dopamine (another feel good brain chemical).

CORTISON - frizzled, frazzled, and stressed out, highly sensitive, physically and emotionally.

VASOPRESSIN – secretive, in the background, subtle, aggressive male energies, brother to testosterone, and brother to oxytocin (makes you want to connect in an active, male way as does oxytocin).

DHEA – reservoir of all the hormones, omnipresent, pervasive sustaining, mist of life, energising, father and mother of testosterone and estrogen, nicknamed "the mother hormone", the Zeus and Hera of hormones and is robustly present in youth and wanes to nothing in older age.

ADROSTENEDIONE – the mother of testosterone in the ovaries supply of sassiness; high spirited in youth, wanes at menopause dies with the ovaries.

ACCOPER GNENOCONE – the luxurious, soothing, mellowing daughter of progesterone, without her we are crabby. She is sedating, calming, easing, neutralises any stress, but as soon as she leaves, all is irritable withdrawal; her sudden departure is the central story of PMS, the three or four days before a woman's period starts.

The Future of Female Brain

Even though there are now proven scientific differences between men and women brains. This in many ways is the Priceless Golden Age for women. The age of Aristotle, Socrates and Plato was the first time in western history that men gained enough resources to have the leisure for intellectual and scientific pursuits. The twenty first century is the first time in history that women are in a similar position. We have not only the critical unprecedented economic means in a networked economy. Scientific advances in women's fertility have given no enormous options. We can now choose when, if and how to have children over many more years of our lives. We are no longer economically dependent on men, and technology has provided the flexibility to toggle between professional and domestic duties, at the time and the same place.

These options give women the gift of using their female brains to create a new paradigm for the way they manage their professional, reproductive and personal lives.

We are living in the midst of a revolution in consciousness about women's biological reality that will transform human society. I cannot predict the exact nature of the change, but I suspect it will be a shift from simplistic to deep thinking about the changes we need to make on a grand scale. If external reality is the sum total, of the way people conceive it, then our external really will change only when the dominant view of it changes. The scientific facts behind how female brain functions perceives reality, respond to emotions, reads emotions in others and nurtures and cares for others are women's reality. Their needs for functioning at their full potential and using the innate talent of female brain are becoming clear scientifically. Women have biological imperative for insisting that a neo-social contract take them and their needs into account. Our future and our children's future depends on it.[14]

Most persuasive however, is the consistent theme of this book, women make fewer errors and are less corrupt, more conscientious, more effective with their work and risk taker together this creates a compelling case for women and only now we can see the full effect their superiority and they prove they are the superior gender.[15]

The women are in men's jobs and are proving themselves better than men, for e.g. Oprah. They know how to solve problems and work together as a team. They spend their money for social causes and also earn money more than man and their priority is client. They focus on people and they are not afraid of their bosses contrary to stereo type. Now they are doing / building empires from computer to banking modern women wants to accomplish everything they know how to achieve will the time and energy. They want the world preserve safe for everybody so politics is safe in their hands. Women are the better future for the world.[16]

Now in Mathematics and Medicine women are doing better than men as a decade. Computer Software to the games they are proving themselves better than men. Naturally, women are nice person but men say they are timid and girly they behave in an angry manner ready to fight for various causes and men call them Iron Lady. They also do not prefer teaching women surgery. That is how men are but now we see women in every field.

The old gentlemen club sexual harassment that makes the workplace hostile and fragile. Women should unite is to defy men of any harassment and create a safe environment to live. For a husband of a modern woman, she is everything that his mother was not.

Equal law and education and economic bring gender superiority. Women understand human feeling better just looking at them so solving problem is easy for them.[17]

Sometimes, it takes one woman; sometimes, it takes many. Almost always, I've found, when in the room; so that everyone stops counting, women become free to ask like women. Its then that we can eliminate double standards and accept that men and women are different and that they bring a different range of experiences, skills and strengths to public life. Its then that we can start to value women as much as men and to retool our institution to fit the broad range of choices that women and men make.

It's then that we can expand our definition of leadership and of the language we use to describe it. It's then that we'll have more representative government, better schools, and more effective diplomacy. We'll have stronger communities and a fairer society. We'll be able to reduce conflict and build a better future.

It's then that we can take advantage of all that each of us has to offer and it is then that women will rule the world. And when women rule we will have changed the very definition of power, we will have changed the world.[18]

Women's Movements

Begum Syeda Abida Hussain, Chairman of the Jhang District Council and the sole directly elected female member of the National Assembly, said that women in Pakistan were in the midst of fighting the biggest *jihad* (holy war) in history, and that "Islam enjoins rights and responsibilities on Muslim women who are not subject to any dispute". Begum Syeda Abida Hussain is currently the Pakistan Ambassador to the United States. The ensuing protests delayed promulgation of the Qanoon-e-Shahdat for nearly two years, and resulted in the final version which called for the testimony of two women begin equal to that of one man in financial cases. In other instances, acceptance of one woman's testimony has been left to the discretion of the presiding judge.

Women's Action Forum

An important break with the past occurred when women themselves organised groups such as Khawteen Mahaz-e-Amal (Women's Action Forum - WAF), the Pakistan Women's Lawyers' Association (PWLA) and the Business and Professional Women's Association in the early 1980s. This was followed by the establishment of research-oriented activist groups, such as the Aurat Foundation, Simorgh and Shirkat Gah. These groups – headed by women - prompted unprecedented private and public discourse about the position of women in Islam and women's roles in a modern Islamic state. Significantly, they revealed the inherent controversy emerging in Pakistan's rapidly changing society: whether or not women and men were to be regarded by the state as equal economic actors and the extent to which parliamentary and civil rights found in the West are applicable in a modern Muslim context.

Perhaps the most important women's group which has facilitated the transformation of the larger women's movement in Pakistan is the Women's Action Forum (WAF), or Khawateen Mahaz-e-Amal. The WAF was organised in 1981 by women in Karachi, Lahore and Islamabad on the principal of collective discriminatory laws and to strengthen women's position in the society. It provided a venue for women, most of them from elite families, to band together and formulate policy statements as well as engage in political action to safeguard women legal position.

The researcher has, therefore, not dealt with the Constitutional provisions at length. Since the legal framework is not able to bring justice it is relevant to take into account how the women are being treated in practice in the name of Qur'an and Sunna. Some modern scholars like late Asghar Ali Engineer and Qamruddin Khan are speaking and writing that the source of the problem is interpretation and understanding of Qur'an and primarily the bias of men, their chauvinism that makes men to take into consideration only a couple of lines not the whole paragraph or the whole Qur'an and use it in favour of men. For example, polygamy is allowed in only extreme conditions and with the condition that all of them be equally treated and that the husband should not stay with only one. At the time when Islam came men used to have hundreds and thousands of wives. When Qur'an was written it attempted to immediately reduce the number to four and promoted one. Muslim men started using half sentence of the Qur'an to their advantage. But now women can read and write they are highly educated so they themselves read Qur'an and learn the truth and stop playing in the hands of men.[19]

During the middle ages in Arabia and Persia and India, the Islamic thinkers and scholars were adding their feelings and norms of that time in their writing of Sharia. Whoever was writing and studying, they had their own experiences and intellect and above all their social and economical conditions and political conditions which influenced and structured their thinking and writing. This can be illustrated by the example of one word in the Qur'an verse chapter 4:34 is 'qawwamun' and this is a very controversial word. In the beginning it was interpreted 'Lord', 'Master', or 'Ruler', and then it became 'Governor' or 'Manager'. This meaning created and over lordship of men and led to subordination of women and dictated to women how to behave in a conditioned society. But Riffat Hassan took the came word into new era and made it "bread winners". She says, "There are many authorities on the basis of whom I can say that it means "bread winner" and it is an economic term ... the interpretation of entire verse changes. It's talking about division of functions, that while women have the primary responsibility of being child bearers... during that time... they should not have the obligation to be bread winners, and therefore men should be breadwinners during this period". Interpretations are human not divine; as soon as we learn this thing there will be change in Pakistan. Here two suras from Qur'an make it clear that women shall benefit from what they earn. And when she is divorced maintenance should be provided. (2:241), "For divorced women maintenance should be provided on a reasonable scale, this is a duty of the righteous".[20]

The same discrimination against women is experienced in the provisions related to the question of the controversial witness. It has been accepted that a woman is worth half a man and woman cannot give witness according to Shariah. However, this man-made Shariah is not what 'Qur'an' intended. If a woman or a thousand women witnesses a murder or rape, the court does not allow these women Qur'an wanted these people be punished to highest degree of punishments. The punishment of the death penalty is prescribed in Qur'an for these men. There are nine verses in Qur'an dealing with witnesses. However, when the male scholars want to prove male superiority they choose one verse which deals only with financial matters. Qur'an verse 2: 282

– "O believers, when you contract a debt one upon another for a slated term, write it down. And call in two witnesses, men or if two be not men, then one man and two women, such witnesses as you approve of, that if one of the two women errs the other will remind her.

"Here the men who the women declare that she is half man and has no right to be witness for Hudood cases and she has no right are judged. She has no right to be her own guardian. This verse is just for loan purposes and at that time to remind her if she forgot. The other woman was not witness. One women and only one woman was witness, other women helping the first.[21]

(1) 5:106 – "O believers, the testimony between you and when any of you is visited by death, at the bequest a thing, shall be two persons equity from among you, or two others from among others that you, if you are journeying in the land and the affliction of death befalls you".

(2) 5:107 – "But if it be discovered that both of them have merited the accusation of any sin, then two others shall stand in their place, these being the nearest of those most concerned". This verse is clarifying that is the previous witness proved to be telling a lie or cheating then the two close relatives or friends come up and become witness. So here it is clear that witnesses are not men or women. They can be any person, a man or a woman.

(3) 65: 1, 2 – "O Prophet, when you divorce women, divorce them when they have reached their period... then when they have reached their term, retain them honourable or part from them honourably. And call into witnesses two persons of equity from among yourselves". Here two persons are not men. Thus in important matters in our life like divorce, also two persons, not necessarily males participate.

(4) 41: 15 "Such of your women as commit indecency, call four of you to witness against them". This one is very serious charge and this requires four witness, men or women.

(5) 24: 4, "And those who accuse chaste women, and then bring not four witnesses, encourage them with eighty stripes."

(6) 24:13 – "Why did they not bring four witnesses against it? But since they did not bring the witnesses, in God's sight they are the liars".

Here it is clear that God wants to save the "Chaste Women" from unwanted accusation so here it is clear that the crime is punishable with 80 whips. However, the Pakistani law-makers have changes this sura and now when women go to jail and receive 80 whips, because she is degrading a "Chaste Man" who may be a rapist or a murderer or both. If the woman is unable to get the witness, it is presumed that she is unnecessarily blaming a 'chaste man' and therefore receives the severe physical punishment of 80 whips.

In the case of divorce, following suras are mentioned –

(1) 24:6 – "And those who excuse their wives and have no witnesses except themselves, the testimony of one of them shall be to testify by God four times that he is of the truthful, and a fifth time, that the curse of God shall be upon him, if he should be of the liars. Court cannot deliver any verdict without hearing the wife.

(2) 24:7 – "It shall avert from the chastisement if she testify by God four times that is the liar, and a fifth time that the wrath of God shall be upon, if he should be of the truthful".

After this court will give them divorce and they will be treated equal parties. Te word "Shariah" is originally came into one of the Qur'anic verses – 45:18 "We have established you on Shariah to adhere to it and not to follow the desire those who know not" here Quran is telling everybody who believe that follow Quran not people who has no knowledge or a little knowledge, people who hide and use only whatever in their favour and make it like their favour and make it like their customs and traditions.[22]

Hudood laws and criminal laws and describe in, Quran every country and every generation define it is own way of understanding and thinking and public follow them. These laws required strict proof and false testimony is a major sin and crime. If a Hud is proof then court as to deliver strict punishment. But before appearing in the court people can forgive or have some other settlement and forgiveness is regarded highly in the eye of God.

Dr Muhammad Ata is one of the modern scholars of Islam and he wants to approach everything with a new perspective. He is rightly points out that the women of today are not confined to the four walls of the home, are educated and have all kind of jobs and are also taking care of the family and themselves. Women have to go out to learn, teach and pursue any job they want, or any career they choose. So today women deserve that her testimony in anything, especially for Hudood crimes should be credible. This is important for a healthy society. He points out that if a rape or murder occurs in the presence of only girls or women, then it does not matter how many girls saw the crime, the criminal will go free. In such circumstances, there cannot be a safe society. "This is too irrational to be accepted as a rule of Islamic evidence" Arabic word, "Minkum" can apply to any group of people men, women or both[5] and is being wrongly interpreted to deny the right of testimony to the women.[23]

Islam did not intend to suppress women or give them a derogatory position. This can be supported with the help of two references in the early phase of development of Islam / Islamic history. The woman, Hafsa, prophet's wife and daughter of Umar was chosen to keep the manuscripts of Qur'an safe and she did successfully. When Caliph Usman asked her to give him the Qur'an, so he should print it for everybody to read, nobody questioned her credibility – they did not doubt her ability to safeguard it or that she would change any part of it. Nobody dared to ask these questions. The other example of the power of women was that of Hazrat Ayesha, was not only the best teacher of Qur'an and Sunnah, but when it was needed she was ready to command an army. When her army was marching from Mecca to Basra she was followed by a big army of men and big sahaba like Zubair and Talha. Very few Muslims know about this history. Both Shia and Sunni distort this fact and minimise her role as commander-in-chief. Inspite of these historical proofs of their ability in political fields the women in Pakistan have no equality in law and are still waiting to go to mosque and pray.[24]

It can be concluded that in India and Pakistan women are trying their best to gain gender equality. It is true that constitutions grant equal legal status and all political rights to both genders including the right to vote. However, the success of any democracy depends on the actual participation of all citizens – men and women.

Ex-President of the USA, Bill Clinton has spoken about the Heifer International:

"Next door to my library in Little Rock, Arkansas, is the world headquarters of Heifer International, founded in 1944 by Dan West, who was a relief worker during the Spanish Civil War. That experience convinced him that what poor and suffering people really need far more that temporary help is the ability to support themselves. So he began shipping them cows. Sixty three years later, Heifer has evolved into one of world's most successful and widely acclaimed givers for two reasons. First, it works to end world hunger by giving cows, goats and other food and income – producing livestock and agricultural goods to poor families around the world. The animals are now bought locally to maximise resistance to local economies. They produce milk, eggs, wool, and meat, enhancing nutrition and earning money for education, health- care, better housing, and small-business endeavours. Heifer partners with local groups to ensure that the agriculture it supports is sustainable, promoting animal health, and water quality, soil conservation, and efficient energy use. Heifer also champions equality for women and community development.

Fittingly, because of its commitment to a sustainable environment, the new international headquarters was built making maximum use of recycled materials, capturing and using rainwater, and conserving energy. I believe that the Heifer headquarters and my library, which has LEED (Leadership in Energy and Environment Design) silver certification from the U.S. Green Building Council, will soon be the only two adjacent headquarters building in America to receive one of the top two LEED certifications.

The second reason for Heifer's success is that those who receive its animals are required to share the first offspring with others in need, thus multiplying the impact of all donated animals and making their recipients partners in the struggle against hunger and poverty. Since 1944, Heifer has given animals to 10 million people, but through the ritual of "Passing on the Gift", it has helped more than 45 million people in 128 countries around the world, with plans to reach 23 million more by the end of the decade. Heifer's message and methods go out to millions of others every year through the media, its own publications, and its three learning centres in the United States, where fifty thousand people annually are taught how to serve small farmers through teaching sustainable practices like organic gardening and alternative marketing methods.

When I spoke at the dedication of the Heifer World Headquarters in 2006, one of the beneficiaries in the audience was Beatrice Biira of Kissinga, a small village on the equator in western Uganda. In the early 1990s, Beatrice, her parents, and five brothers and sisters were struggling to survive when they received on of twelve goats Heifer donated to Kissinga. Beatrice had always wanted to go to school, but her family was too poor to afford the school fees. Within a year her mother had earned enough money selling goat's milk to pay the fees. Eventually she was able to send all the rest of her children to school with her earnings from selling milk and the goat's offspring (after passing on the gift of the first one). Beatrice completed her first three grades in three months each, showing such promise that Dick Young, producer of a Heifer documentary film that featured her village, helped pay for her enrollment at a more advanced school in Kampala, Uganda's capital. From there she went for a year to a prestigious American prep school, Northfield Mount Hermon in Massachusetts, then on to Connecticut College on a scholarship. While there, Beatrice served as an intern in Hillary's Senate office. She has been featured on *60 Minutes* and by Oprah Winfrey, a Heifer supporter. Her remarkable story is chronicled in *Beatrice's Goat,* an engaging children's book written by Page McBrier and illustrated by Lori Lohstoeter. Beatrice wants to go home and use her education to benefit her people by forming a school for poor kids, taking care of AIDS orphans, or running a farm that helps other children the way Heifer helped her and her family. It all began with a goat called Mugisa (Which means "Luck").

A Nepalese Women's group, Gurung Gaon, used a Heifer water buffalo to improve their lot. Beyond passing on the offspring, the women saved enough of their income to buy one hundred geese for five families in China. Women in a Heifer project in Zimbabwe passed on twice as many pigs as required because they wanted more women to enjoy the same prosperity they did.[25]

We see how women once again prove their superiority in diverse conditions to reach out and help others in need.

3

World Religion

World religion speaks about same language to put women down. They all say to put women in their place

Most men want to put women in their place... so they are denied for any rights – political, economical, social, religious or educational.

Social and Religious Practices in India and Pakistan

The human population in the country is basically conditioned by the societal customs and traditions. At the same time the religious beliefs of the people dominate and at times totally determine the social practice. Gender itself is a social construct which has now completely over shadowed the biological distinction of sexes. Consequently, it is often seen that the status and role of women in any country is greatly dependent on its social system and religious practices. It is therefore, essential to understand the influence of social practices and in order to comprehend the status of women in any country.

The women of India and Pakistan seem to be living in a tragic and painful circle of life where they are not aware of their rights. They struggle daily for food, water, fuel, childbirth and child rearing without any help. Men define their social role for them and it has been well established through centuries of rules and regulations supported by religious leaders. They have no part in decision-making of any kind, so they have low self-esteem. Their work has no financial value. All their life, they remain subordinate to their fathers, husbands and in later years even their sons. Since the whole condition demands a change in the attitude of men towards women, society will change along with men. The ideology of particular interest keeps women in their place again and again. Religion and culture celebrate women as self-sacrificing wives and mothers. As a result the entire social set up is working against women's rights.[1]

INDIA

In India there is a deep difference between the reference of the status of women in various scriptures and religious texts and the real status of women. On the one hand, they are termed as *'devi'* or goddess and regarded as 'worthy of worship', and on the other hand, they are burnt for dowry, cursed for being witches, brutally beaten by the men in the family.

Women are deeply respected in religious references and the scripts and received high in *Vedic* and Pre-*Vedic* period. However, for ages they have been suffering social prejudice and labeled disabilities in the past. The socio-cultural set up in India has idolised a woman for her role as a 'mother' and 'care-taker' but the woman is not projected as a 'bread winner', 'decision-maker' or 'leader'. This role prefers to keep them imprisoned within the four walls of household.

When the history of women's condition in the various ages is seen, it is witnessed that women enjoyed rights in education, religion, politics and property equal to that of men in the *Vedic* period. In the *Atharva Veda* it is recited that the newly-wed bride is the queen of the house of her in-laws and her in-laws should live in joy and peace under her region there. The women were also said to have contributed to the economic growth of the society. In the later *Vedic* period women enjoyed with men in social and economic fields. *Bhishma pitamah* had said that women should be treated with affection and reverence but she should not be treated as a demi-goddess and put into confinement of dwelling. In the *Manu Smriti* the freedom of women was put under checks.

The later *Vedic* period showed that certain attributes of women such as their shy nature, feeling of mercy, pity and compassion were regarded as their weakness and the men started exploiting them. The decline of the social status of women enhanced during the medieval times. Under the Mughals most of the people were living a happy life and India was the bird of gold. The Mughal's wife and their mother ruled side by side with them. During the British colonial rule India became the poorest country.

Raising the status of women was necessary in developing a new society and the concept of 'new woman' emerged in the nineteenth century. However, in practice the British did nothing to enhance the social status of women in India. The British never cared about India or the Indians. They gave Indians the status of dogs and slaves. Their emphasis was on teaching the English language and dressing styles to the Indian women who accompany their Indian officer husbands when they were with British officers. In the economic field they suffered with several inabilities. In the joint family system the women did not receive their shares into the parental property. If woman was born in a respectful family she was not supposed to go out of her home for work. Her high birth prevented her from earning money for her own upkeep. The women came forward to extend their help in the national movement. Under the leadership of Gandhiji they were effective in the programmes of picketing and alcoholism. The women in large numbers worked shoulder to shoulder with men during India's struggle against the British.

In India the leaders have advocated the significance of family of women but have not distinctly promoted women's rights. Mahatma Gandhi promoted the age old image of women with no self-interest. He showed respect for the women who were willing to sacrifice. He said, "To me, the female sex is not the weaker sex. It is the nobler of the two for it is even today the embodiment of sacrifice, silent suffering, humility, faith and knowledge." In 1963, Sarojini Naidu appealed to women to work for their livelihood, though male leaders wanted women to stay home. The social reforms during the national movement after independence were not able to help the masses of poor women in India. They only helped the upper caste Hindu women.[2]

Under the British, Indian became the poorest country in the world and everybody was considered as British slaves. British never care about India or Indians. Status of women went down even more. The Moghul women had the power and India was called the bird of gold, but now it became the poorest country and they become miserable slaves. After 200 years of rule and every 50 years, Hindu and Muslim communities fought with the British under the command of Moghul. After 100 years when the Moghuls were fighting against the British, the British killed every child belonging to Moghul families, so that no Moghul family can come and rule India again. When India became Independent, the British separated India and Pakistan. India wanted somebody to hold them together. After Independence Nehru tried to rule like the Moghuls, but it was not possible and women's condition became worst in 60 years.

Now, for the real history of 3000 years and more, Indians must read from *Humayun Naman* by the first Moghul Emperor, and Moghul History as documented by Bahadur Shah Zafar, the last Mughal Emperor. He wrote very sad poetry, when he was jailed and died under the British rule.

Muslim women have to move forward when other religion know to give women equal rights. Most of the Muslim countries are doing worst war against women who are in slavery. No education, no job in today's modern world. All men seem to agree with the religious topic that women should be second to them.

Sharia law is not Koran it is a British law for Muslim women. If any man or woman say against it they will kill her like the extremists tried to do with Malala of Pakistan. We women have to be fearless like her.

Women have to be Educated and Learn Self-defense

Everywhere in the world women go to mosque. In India and Pakistan, they don't go to mosque, whereas they are allowed to pray in Church, Gurudwara, or temple but not in a mosque.

The civilisation that worshipped the Goddess, which had flourished for 1000's of years bringing with them in earliest times inventions in methods of agriculture, medicine, architecture, textiles, wheeled vehicles, ceramics, metallurgy and written language, were gradually stamped out. Though the Indo-Europeans had initiated a great many changes, it was later the duty of every He brew and then of every Christian to suppress and destroy the worship of the female deity wherever it still existed. "I have come to destroy the works of the female".[3]

The Abbasids were hardly any different from the Umayyads. The Abbasi did the same with the Muslim women and Qur'an. Though they captured power by projecting themselves as children of uncle of the Prophet, they turned out to be no lesser tyrants. They persecuted members of the Prophet's household (Ahl-al-Bayt), and saw them as competitors for power. They spread a network of spies to trace and kill them. The Abbasid period turned out to be the period of enlightenment for men, as Abbasid rulers took great interest in transferring Greek knowledge and philosophy. So was the case with Indian knowledge and philosophy that were translated into Arabic. This was the main difference between the Umayyads and Abbasids. The Umayyads' power base was primarily Arabs. They were interested only in reviving the pre-Islamic Arab culture and took no interest in non-Arabic knowledge.

The Abbasid power base was mainly non-Arab and distinctly Persian that had a long tradition of learning and culture. They helped Abbasid rulers to find the house of wisdom (Dar-al-Hilemah), wherefrom great treasures of Greek and Indian knowledge and philosophy were translated and disseminated. It was during the Abbasid period that various school of Shariah laws came to be compiled.[4]

Shariah law is nowhere in Quran. These laws are totally against women and the superiority of women in the Quran. This is the beginning of Islam men doing everything against Quran to prove them to be superior to women. After 1000 years women have awakened. No more will men make laws to oppress women. We all need to stand up against it.

Persons like Mahatma Gandhi, who undoubtedly had a very deep conviction for non-violence, failed to create violence free India. Independence accompanied by Partition, saw unprecedented violence. Yet he is known as the Apostle of non-violence. Much before him, Christ is known as prince of peace and love, ended violently himself nor his followers except for first three centuries, during which they were a highly persecuted minority, remain peaceful and even Church participated in crusades, bringing about killing of thousands of innocent people or church even allowed burning at stakes of all those who deviated from the Church.

To create a non-violent society we need to create a just society and creating a just society evokes at times rivers of blood as it happened in Muslim history (which I do not refer to as Islamic history as it creates needless confusion). This was deliberately or otherwise, a result of Islamic teachings and some Muslim scholars and historians are no less responsible for this. Jihad became much misunderstood word.

In the light of all this as we turn to the Prophet of Islam to study his convictions, struggle can be divided into two main phases. First the Meccan phase – from his birth to his migration to Medina – which became his ultimate resting point and second his stay in Medina until death. The Prophet an honest, trustworthy, peaceful non-violent person on coming to Mecca was greatly distressed to see the turmoil social anarchy, class differences between poor and disposed and slavery added to that for which he resorted to isolate himself in a cave known as a cave of Hira on the outskirts of Mecca. Here, he contemplated and prayed to God for hours and days altogether but, he was no recluse. He prayed to God to show him the way. His wife Khadija, who was 15 years senior to him, accepted him as a Prophet and congratulated him.[5]

Today thanks to Al-Qaeda and Taliban, Islam has been reduced to killing innocent people to gain power and wealth. There should be strong opposition and all sources encouraging such bloodshed must stop. Though it is too late but even now Ulema from Islamic world must come out strongly in opposition to such gross misuse of Islam in contemporary period. The Muslim Ulema should also draw up charter of ethics and give it wide publicity to alienate these terrorists from Muslim masses. To remain silent in the face of such horrific killings is to be part of it.[6]

The ladies of the Mughal palaces were proficient in both horsemanship and social etiquettes and were also often astute politicians and artists. Akbar's mother, Hamida Banu Begum, was capable advisor both to her husband and son.

Akbar's wife, Jodha (Rajput), was also endowed with superb mental powers and natural ability. The woman writer Gulbadan Begum has been immortalised by her facile pen, while Nur Jahan's role as the power behind Jahangir's throne need not be repeated here. Mumtaz Mahal, Sahajahan's wife, was the Emperor's leading counsellor, and after her death her place was taken by their daughter, Jahan Ara.

The birth of a son was deemed a blessing by both Hindus and Muslims. Girls were unwelcome. Although the Rajputs took many wives, they consider girl babies a curse, and female infanticide was widespread. Both Hindu and Muslim married off their children at an early age without their consent. Dowry was essential for girls and was a great strain on a family. It was a wrong history reported that many Muslims with several daughters were full of praise for *sati* (the Hindu custom of incinerating widows on their husband's funeral pyres). However, Muslims like Batula, were shocked to see the enthusiasm at these *sati* scenes. Akbar's ordinance forbidding the forcible burning of Hindu widows was not strictly obeyed.

This is wrong history that Mughal hated India. All Mughals loved peace with Hindus and others from first to last. The Mughals loved India and the Hindus. They were here with the Hindus for 3000 years of Mughal rule in India.

"Prime Minister Narendra Modi please read the real Mughal Indian History".

Mughals were fighting the British right from the start. The British killed all the Mughals including children and when the last Mughal Emperor was killed and the Mughal were fighting for free India until the dynasty were all killed by the British. The Congress was formed by Muslim women. Only Muslim women were trying to free India for all 22 states, but the Hindus were fighting for only their own states. A Muslim woman whose child was hanged by the British first started the movement. Then Jinnah and Nehru started the struggle for Independent India (Modern India). Hindus and Muslims were all together in the struggle. Men and women alike joined in the fight for freedom. But the British brought division between Hindus and Muslims. Here came Mahatma Gandhi, who said no fighting the British only disobedience and no-violence and there was going back to 'Ram Rajya' for India. Of course, British was not very happy.

They did not want any country as powerful as them. With Hindu-Muslim unity, India could become as powerful and peaceful as it was during the Mughals era, 'The Bird of Gold'.

Before giving India Independence the British changed the Mughal History and made it appear that because of the Mughals India was a poor country, but they were known as the most powerful empire. The wrong history has broken the Hindu and Muslim unity. For the British know that with their unity India can become stronger than them, but a divided India will be weak. We need to re-read history to, for without the Hindu-Muslim unity, India cannot become a powerful nation.

Hindu and Muslim masses as well as classes had developed common ways of life. A Bengali Muslim and a Bengali Hindu had much more in common than Bengali Muslim and a Punjabi Muslim had. Moreover, Hindus and Muslims were being equally and jointly oppressed and exploited by British Imperialism.

Here is an example of the facts known of only a few specific cases, which have occurred in Saudi Arabia, over the last several years:

1. Sri Lankan domestic worker (male) was sentenced to one year in jail and 100 lashes for practicing black magic, although no one showed any specific examples what kind of black magic he practiced.

2. A second Sri Lankan citizen this time a woman was arrested on suspicion of practicing witchcraft, after she stared too long at a child in the shopping centre. She was wearing a black cord around her wrist, which was found by the judge to imply that she must be a witch. Her punishment is unknown as of this writing.

3. A Saudi woman named Amina bint Abdul Halim bi Salem Nasser was executed for committing sorcery and witchcraft, although the specific deeds she committed have

not been made public. Members of the committee made a simple statement that Ms. Nasser was a threat to Islam.

4. A Saudi man, named Muree bin Ali bin Issa La-Asira, was falsely reported as committing sorcery. When various books and talisman were found in his home, he was arrested, tried and beheaded in the southern Najran province.

5. A Saudi woman aged 60 years was beheaded for witchcraft after tricking people into giving her money after she claimed she could heal them of sicknesses.

6. Mustafa Ibrahim, an Egyptian man, was beheaded after he was accused of casting spells to try to separate a married couple. The judge said, he was convinced of Mustafa's guilt after the discovery in Mustafa's home of candles, foul smelling herbs and books.

7. A famous case involving a Muslim Lebanese citizen has been made known worldwide only because the Lebanese government fought for his release and his story made the news. The man named Ali Hussain Saibat, was the TV host of a popular show in Lebanese called "The Hidden". The show was a reality psychic hot line. Mr Saibat gave advice to the members of the audience and sometimes cast a few spells. This show had obviously caught the attention of the Saudi religious police because when Saibat travelled to Saudi Arabia for pilgrimage he was arrested on charges of sorcery. Although he was not a Saudi citizen and his crimes had occurred in another country, it did not stop the anti-witchcraft unit feeling themselves the keepers of the faith not only in Saudi Arabia but all around the world, they took Sibat for trial and won a guilty verdict from the judge. Mr. Sibat was sentenced to beheading. The date was set several times over the course of several years, but each time the date arrived, the Lebanese government succeeded in stopping the execution. Although it is believed that Sibat has not

been beheaded, the Saudi government will not say if he has been released or is still in prison or back home in Lebanon. If he has been released, he has been quiet publicly, although I am certain that in private he is especially stridently about the barbarity of my country. Kareem promise to determine his fate and the moment he does I will make his fate public.

8. An Eritrean man was arrested and imprisoned after his leather telephone address book was confiscated and presented to the court as a talisman because the religious police could not read the man's foreign writing and believed that the booklet was filled with chants that would cause men to leave their wives or wives to leave their husbands. The poor man must have been confuse and terrified, for he was not given an attorney and all the proceedings were in a language he did not understand, although his telephone booklet was held up and pounded on the table and was the cause for his imprisonment and punishment of hundreds of lashes.

9. Sudanese Abdul Hamid bin Hussein Moustafa al-Fakki was the victim of a sting operation where an undercover agent working for the committee asked him to create a spell that would make his father leave his second wife. The undercover agent swore Al-Fakki could do it, but for a charge of $1,500. No one knows of course if this is the case, as the religious authorities are so eager to arrest, flog and even behead people, who can trust their testimony.

10. Lastly, a poor woman was trapped by a female undercover agent who asked the woman if she might turn her husband into an obedient man. Supposedly, the woman said she could, and she was promptly arrested and later sentenced to death.

"The greatest of all riches is education, while the great wealth can be lost, education cannot be withdrawn or cancelled or recalled. Education multiplies like no other investment because it encourages a hunger that is never satisfied. This is why I have spent much of my adult life spreading the idea that education is wealth".[7]

Society condemns when women are raped, without being any of her faults. Nobody stands by them, sometimes not even their own mothers. They suffer the punishment and ostracism all their lives both physically and emotionally. And above all, there is no justice for them. Only if male-dominated society changes its attitude towards women, can woman enjoy their fundamental rights of equality. A husband's right over his wife is absolute in India. It is difficult to imagine a wife crying that her husband has raped her. It does not matter even if she is a minor. India has laws against marital rape, but because of societal standards, wives are neither willing nor do they have the means to go to court[8].

Divorce is allowed legally, but is not approved by the society. Marriage is not a contract but religious duty and is considered to be an alliance trans-life. Women not only in this life, but in all seven lives should pray for the same husband.

4

Women's Rights and Superiority in Sixth Century

What happened to women's rights that Qur'an gave in Sixth century?

Qur'an Vs Hadees – when mullas talk they think they know but it is bad interpretation by men.

At the end of the world God call men and women by their mothers name and not by the father's name.

The Prophet says :

"Your heaven is under your mother's feet. When both mother and father call you at same time for the seventh time you go to mother and the eighth time you go to father".

Hajj Rules

- They need to pray with husband. Same for men and women there, why not in India.
- Hold hands and pray together in Hajj
- Nobody can hide their faces during Hajj

Hijab Covering the Face

According to Qur'an men and women have to lower their gaze when they have to go out in public. If the woman has to cover herself from top to toe there would be no point in the man lowering his gaze. This would imply that woman would keep their face uncovered hence the men have to cover their gaze and not chase them with their eyes. If Qur'an is telling both men and women to lower their gaze in each other's presence, the implication is that the woman is not veiled on her face, otherwise what is there to lower your eyes from? During the Hajj pilgrimage it is specifically forbidden for a woman to cover her face with a veil.

Qur'an disagrees on accumulation and storing of wealth. It, in fact, insists that the wealth that belongs in excess to the society that is collected be distributed to the weaker sections of the society. Also in order to avoid extremes of violence as justice is the key concept of Qur'an, for it allows gradual redistribution of the wealth.

The Qur'an specifically states its stand in favouring the weaker section as quoted – *"And we wished to be gracious to those who were being weakened in the land, and to make them leaders and to make them inheritors (of this earth)" (28:25).*

It also makes it clear that wealth should not be circulated only among the rich (59:7).

Even in view of the punishments, the Qur'an tones down its effect on the weaker section considering the circumstances as situation or background, because of which the act is carried out.

The Qur'an there hopes in person, who believes in Qur'anic message as a medium to bring about justice in the entire society thus transforming it into a peaceable ambience to live and exist in, The Prophet has said,

"The believer is a new type of human being, a new creation who would now endeavour in the project of establishing social justice on God's earth and would not adhere under any circumstances, to injustice in any form. He / she would strive

into the very end to establish a just society. He/she would not be fearful and restrain him/herself from standing up for the truth and speak even if he/she confronts the most unjust tyrannical rules. This would exemplify as the best form of jihad (holy war)".

The real motive or thought of jihad was not to spread Islam at the point of a sword. The real intention made mention in Qur'an was with an understanding of *jihad* was to fight persecution and corruption on the Earth and to cleanse it from these evils.

Therefore, as quoted in the Qur'an which says, *"And fight them on until there is no more tumult of oppressor, and there prevail justice and faith in God. But if they cease, let there be no hostility except to those (sic) practice specifically indicates that* jihad *is only meant to fight or oppose oppression and exploitation. The hostilities/violence can cease with those who perpetrate oppression and persecution (illai ala al-za"dimin)".*

Therefore a believer is a mujahid (a fighter) in the cause of justice. And one who believes and understands justice is being oppressed or exploited. The believer has to extend him/herself to the cause of justice. As he/she is called to worship truly in complete devotion towards God, that is true *'ibadat'*.

God is compassionate and therefore the one who believes and worships God as a true worshipper would imbibe in him/her, the same attributes that are in God. Hence, they are therefore enabled by God's compassion to deliver justice to the weaker sections of the society and the ones that are oppressed and exploited.

Abada God means to adore God and one who adores God would oneself imbibe in themselves the ways of God. Another description of *abada* means is to pave a way (road). Thus, the real *ibada* means is to create or enabling the individual to form or live as a society as fearless beings away from being subject to oppression, being exploited and living harmoniously.

More emphasis to this perspective according to Qur'an is that God intended humankind to be an inhabitant of being created by God, the expression of God's love.

It is said and I quote, *"O humankind! We have created you from a single (pair) of a male and a female, made you into nations and tribes, that ye may know each other (not that ye may despise each other) verily that most honourable of you in the sight of God is (who is) the most righteous of you". (49:13)*

These expressions of God shed light and clear all misconceptions being created. God addressing the whole mankind clarified that all were made and not any specific kind. God further emphasises on creating (making) us as equals (male and female). Also stating later that we were divided as nations and tribes not to rule and have superiority over each other but to acknowledge each other only for the single purpose that God made us as the most superior and most honoured of all creation.

Man's jealousy of woman's capacity to bear children is nowhere better exhibited than in the Old Testament creation story in which man is caused to give birth (from one of ribs) to woman.

"And the rib, made He a woman, and brought her unto the man". (Genesis 2:22)

A frequent subject of medieval art is the birth of Eve from Adam's side. Milton considered the creation of woman a mistake about which he wrote in "Paradise Lost".

We begin to see then that child birth, as well as menstruation was transformed from perfectly healthy natural phenomena into a handicap and a curse. Men project their unconscious wishes upon the screen of their society and create their institutions and gods in the image of their desires. One can deny the virtues of women's advantages by treating them as disadvantages and by them with mysterious or dangerous qualities hence, the tracking down of witches. By making women objects of fear and something to be avoided as unclean, one can reduce the cultural status of women by simple inversion. Their biological advantages are demoted to the status of cultural disadvantages and are demoted to the status of cultural disadvantages; they are then converted into biological disadvantages.

From an early age females have been conditioned to believe that menstruation is a curse and a handicap. Pregnancy, females were taught, put them in a precarious condition, while childbirth was enveloped in so many myths, mysteries and dangers that most women in the western world would have until recently, experienced the event without foreboding and anxiety.

Since the advent of natural childbirth women are finding childbirth far less unpleasant and scarcely handicapping. Childbirth is neither a disease, nor a disorder, nor a handicap. We know today that menstruation is neither mysterious nor malignant, but a perfectly healthy, normal function of woman. Pregnancy needs neither be precarious nor handicapping nor need childbirth or childbearing. Women have been led to believe that these functions are handicapping, and that they must, at best play a secondary role to men. Today, both women and men perhaps better understand how his belief came into being, and perhaps endeavour to make necessary concession to the facts. The malc has everywhere to acquire a broad experience and varied knowledge, which has been denied the female.

Why is it that men, under such conditions consider woman inferior.

In the Torah, Deuteronomy 24:1, the plight of the married woman was made clear. Quote – *"When a man hath taken a wife, and married her, and it come to pass that she find no favour in his eyes, because he hath found some uncleanness in her: then let him write her a bill of divorcement, and give it in her hand, and send her out of his house".*

As we read previously under the Levite law only the husband could as for or demand divorce. In fact, all he had to do was write a note.

Every time we read the Qur'an – *"Bismillah*[1] *ir Rahman ir Rahim*[2]. *It means God is most precious and gracious* [1] *and the womb (mother)* [2] *is blessed (woman's womb),* was not regarded as curse, because of the pain the women go for childbirth. In Qur'an it is called blessed and not cursed. This proves women as superior beings as they are in charge of the human race and not men.

The Sixth Century evidence of Women's Superiority in the Qur'an

Mary and Hagar (Prophets)

Mary (Maryam) the Mother of Prophet Jesus (Isa) in the Quran is a Prophet.

"Mary" is the only female identified in the Qur'an by name. Her name appears in a large number of Qur'anic verses and is also the title of a Sura (Sura 19). Most other personal names used as titles of Qur'anic chapters are those of Prophets. For example: Sura 10 – Yunus; Sura 11 – Hud; Sura 12 – Yusuf; Sura 14 – Ibrahim; Sura 47 – Muhammad; Sura 71 – Nuh.

Before her birth Mary's mother had consecrated her to God's service. After her birth, she invoked God's protection for her and her progeny from Satan. According to authenticated tradition, both Mary and her son Jesus, thereby escaped the pricking of the devil at birth, which tradition is said to have played a role in the formation of the later Islamic doctrine of prophetic *isma* (innate quality of impeccability) "Immunity from sin and error of prophets. Mary served in the *mihrab*, where the conceived miraculous sustenance, while a virgin. God's angels spoke to Mary to give her glad tidings of a word (*kalima*) from God. God cast of the Spirit of God to Mary to give her a pure son. Was Mary then a Qur'anic Prophet?

Suras 19:17; 21:91 and 66:12, state that Mary was impregnated by "Our Spirit". Jesus is identified as God's prophet, the Word that God cast into Mary and a Spirit from God (4:171), Jesus was supported with the Holy Spirit (*ru-uh-qudus*) (2:87, 253; 5:13). The casting of God's spirit into Mary reveals the gift of God's spirit to Adam shaped from clay (15:29; 32:9; 38:72). While Jesus supported by the Holy Spirit recalls the strengthening of those in whose hearts faith is firmly inscribed *"with a spirit from God" (58:22)*. In addition, the Qur'an speaks of the trusted spirit *(al ruh al-amin)* as the agent of God's revelation (26:193; cf 16:102). The spirit is further mentioned together with, but separate from the angels (97:4; 70:4; 78:38) and also as something conveyed by the angels to God's chosen servants (16:2). In its role as conveyor of revelation, the spirit is identified as Gabriel (Jibril) (2:97).

In Mary's story, the spirit is life creating force of, or from God. To this day, however, Islamic exegesis has differentiated between, *"Our (God's) spirit sent to Mary in the form of a man (19:17) and "Our (God's) spirit (of) which we breathed into Mary" (21:91; 66:12).*

While the former has been "personalised" by way of identification with Gabriel, the latter is understood as the life substance with which God (directly) awakened Adam to life from clay, just as it (directly) awakened Jesus to life in Mary's womb. Classical exegesis established that Gabriel was the means of instrument of God's creative power. But contemporary thinkers perpetuate the notion that 'somehow' God's spirit in form of a well shaped human *"qua"*. Gabriel in human form was a different "entity" than the spirit which God breathed (directly) into Mary. The issue has not attracted much further attention. On the whole the conservative sheikhs, familiar with the medieval rationalist tradition are merely imitative of medieval authorities. Others find little use in the scholastic tradition since their attention was with social, economic and political issues, the new agenda of defining Islam in the modern world.

Was Mary a Prophet?

Some Muslim theologians, especially of the Zahirite (literalist) school have argued that Mary mother of Jesus, Sara mother of Isaac, and the mother of Moses are to be reckoned among God's prophets because according to the Qur'an angels spoke to them (or God otherwise inspired them). In a controversial tract, the Zahirite Ibn Hazm of Cordova (date 1064), argued in favour of women's prophethood, but distinguished *nubuwwat* (prophethood) from *risala* (messengerhood) the latter restricted to men. According to the Ibn Hazm, the knowledge the mother of Isaac, Jesus and Moses received from God (through word of inspiration) was as true as the knowledge received by male prophets (through revelation). Ibn Hazm, further likens the "inspiration" of Moses' mother (to throw her son into the river) to Abrahams inspiration (to sacrifice his son). Both would have been crazy as well as sinful in acting on the inspiration unless they trusted its divine source. According to Ibn Hazm, Mary's prophethood is further classified in that the Quran also calls her a *"Woman of Truth" (5:75)* just as it speaks of the prophet Joseph as a *"Man of Truth" (12:46)*.

Finally the authenticated prophetic tradition that Asiya the Pharaoh's wife and Mary are the two perfect women, prompt Ibn Hazm not only to include Asiya among the prophets in the manner that Muhammad and Abraham are ranked among the male.[1]

Let me start by bringing forward clear evidence to create the misconceptions of the spiritual status of women and whether or not they have souls, which might experience Paradise. The Qur'an states categorically that "*men and women who practice the principles of Islam will receive equal reward for their efforts. Surely for men who submit (to God) and for women who submit (to God), for believing men and for believing woman, for devout men and for devout women, for steadfast men and steadfast women, for truthful men and truthful women, for humble men and for humble women, for charitable men and charitable women, for men who fast and for women who fast, for men who guard their chastity and for women who guard their chastity, for men who remember God and for women who remember God – for them God has prepared forgiveness and a mighty reward". (33:35)*

Again God says:

"Whosoever performs good deeds whether male or female and is a believer, we shall surely make him a good life and we will certainly reward them for the best of what they did". (The Qur'an16:97)

Each of the five pillars of Islam, belief, prayer, fasting, poor-due and pilgrimage-is important for a woman as for men and there is no differentiation of their reward. One may also mention that one of the most famous mystics of Islam, Rabi'cal 'Adawiyya, was a woman.

As God says in the Qur'an, *"The noblest among you before God, is the most needful of you". (49:13)*[2]

Intellectual Status

Having established beyond question the spiritual equality of men and women in Islam, what of their intelligence, knowledge and education? The Prophet Muhammad said: *"The search of Knowledge is a duty for every Muslim (male or female).*

"Seek knowledge from the cradle to the grave".

"Knowledge" is not divided into sacred or secular, and the implications of these sayings of the Prophet, in modern terms is that of every Muslim boy or girl, man or woman, should pursue his or her education as far as it is possible, bearable in mind the words of God in Qur'an".

"Only those of His servants, who are learned, truly fear God" (35:28)

In Islam, therefore, men and women are credited with the capacity for learning and understanding and teaching and one of the aims of acquiring knowledge is that of becoming more conscious of God. It is considered in Islam that the more a person male or female studies the creation and observes its workings, the more he or she becomes conscious of the creator, the Power who made and sustains the creation.[3]

As for parents, the Prophet said that when both of your parents are calling you, you answer seven times to your mother and one time to your father. He also said that heaven is under your mother's feet (not the father). So as parents, mother is superior to the father. New research and data shows women are spiritually and intellectually superior to man.

Women and Inheritance

Well traditionally, there was no share in inheritance for daughters Islam created it. Women were not earning and contributing towards the family wealth. She would go to her husband's house and get a share in her husband's property. In addition she would get *mehr* at the time of marriage and also a promise for maintenance. Given all this it would not be injustice if she got only half a share in her father's property.

"In the encyclopedic work Ikhwaras Safa, there is a debate on this issue. The Master tells that Islam gives double of what is intended to others.

The disciples ask, 'Are women among weaker sections?'

The Master said, 'Yes'.

The disciples ask, 'Why women are given only half of what brothers get in father's property?'

Master says, 'You have not understood the Quranic logic of giving half to the daughters. In fact, the Quran has given twice of that of sons'.

Bewildered, the disciples ask, 'How half can be twice?'

The Master explains, 'If the father leaves behind 1000 dirhams, the son will get 500, and the daughter will get 250. When the son will marry, he will give 250 dirham as mehr. And when daughter marries, she will get 250 by way of mehr and will have 250 + 250, i.e. 500 dirham with her whereas her brother has been left with only 250 dirham after giving mehr. Thus who got twice, son or daughter? Obviously, the daughter got".

But, this explanation assumes certain things which may not be true in today's life. First, women may not get substantial *mehr*, at times she gets nominal *mehr*. Secondly, these days the middle class women work and contribute towards the family wealth so she is entitled to a larger share.

Thirdly, in many cases women may not get married. Not only would they not get *mehr*, but they will also have to maintain themselves after their parents', death. Thus, the Ikhwara Safa explanation today is redundant. But the Qur'an is not insensitive and leaves place for justice. The Qur'anic verses on inheritance end with provision that after paying, *"a bequest you may have bequeathed or a debt" (4:11-12)*. The Qur'an repeats this twice. Thus, we see four times the Qur'an lays stress on bequest or debt, if anyone on the part of the deceased and then remaining will go to the inheritors as laid down by the Qur'an. Thus the person who leaves behind the property has every right to make a will in favour of anyone he likes.

The Jurists have argued that these verses on inheritance were revealed.

One finds an interesting discussion on this, in Maulana Umar Ahamd Usmani's book *Giqh-al-Qur'an* seventh volume (*Karachi*, 1986). Thus, the Qur'anic injunction for will stands and the father has every right to will extra in favour of his daughter who cannot or does not want to marry or is physically challenged or maybe is contributing to the family income.[4]

Role of Woman in Karbala

Yazid stood for that which was against Islam. Not only his lifestyle was against that of the Prophet (PBUH) and his companions but he also tried to destroy the institute of Khilafah and Imamat and introduced reactionary institution of monarchy which was totally against the revolutionary political system introduced by Islam. Husain knew before he left for Kufah, what was in store that he deliberately took women along with him to show the world that woman can also play, very important role in saving Islamic revolution. And these women did play a role which was no less significant than that of male companions of the Imam. And Imam was right particularly his Hazrat Zainab took the lead. After the martyrdom of the Imam and his colleagues Imam Zainul Abidi, all women and children were arrested and taken to Damascus on bare camel back via Kufa. Syeda Zainab, a brave and bold woman addressed Muslims everywhere, exposing Yazid and his evil actions and un-Islamic acts and his counter-revolutionary designs.

Syeda Zainab and the Imam's entire family was kept in prison in Damascus and when they were brought to Yazdi's court, Zainab eloquently spoke in front of all Yazid's courtiers and thoroughly exposed him. She never shied away in exposing him so much that he had to release her and Imam's entire family and sent them back to Madina ensuring their security. Syeda Zainab's role was exemplary and it very well showed how bold were Muslim women and how they played the important role in consolidating Islamic revolution. Today, despite so much progress and spread of education still Muslim women are suppressed and in some countries like Saudi Arabia even their voice is considered *awrab* (not be publicly heard) and here Zainab and other women from Imam's family were the main speakers.

Hazrat Zainab was eldest among those women and was leading entire family, including Imam, Zainab Abidin who was then quite sick and unable to play an active role and it was Hazrat Zainab who had to play a leadership role and she proved to be the first among superiors. Today, women have to learn much from her leadership. Her public role and oratorical skills have much to learn from.[5]

Rahmat - The Mercy of God

A key term of the Holy Qur'an is (rahmat), which is translated as mercy or also as compassion. The Qur'an lays great emphasis on compassion. Two of God's names are Rahim and Rehman i.e. Merciful and compassionate or Dispenser of grace. Mercy for God is so fundamental that, *"God has ordained mercy" (6:12)*, which means one cannot think of God without mercy. The Qur'an also describes the Prophet as *Rehmul lil Aalanun* i.e. mercy of the worlds. Thus, both God and the Messenger represent mercy and compassion.

It is quite interesting to note that *rahem* means mother's womb and while in mother's womb it is protected from outside influences. Mother's womb nourishes the foetus and it grows within its protected shell. Thus, God is also nourisher and sustainer of the whole universe. Every species in the universe grows and flourishes under God's protection and because of God's *rehmat*. According to Taj-al-urus, *rahma* is that innate quality which brings about hidden and manifest perfection in a being and it is available freely without any direct or indirect condition. Women Superiority again! [6]

Husband-wife Relationship

- **Giving undue authority to the husband**

Our scholars however ignore these illuminating hadith and have taken nushuz to mean the wife's rebellion against the husband. By emphasising, *"Fear of nashuz"* they have made the husbands subjective judgement the criterion for the three steps mentioned in verse 4:34. At the same time they have taken 4:34 to be the last word on husband and wife relationship. They also take "obedience" here to mean obedience to the husband.

Harshness to women is Haram

In sura nisa, there is evidence against the "husbandly" interpretation of our scholars. The Qur'an here expressly forbids any harsh treatment to women, even if the husband dislikes the wife intensely.

"O you who believe you are forbidden to inherit women against their will. And do not treat them with harshness (la ta du la hunna) that you may take away part of the dower you have given them, except where they have been guilty of open lewdness. On the contrary, live with them with kindness and justice (a' shirunna bil-maraf) even if you dislike them. It may be that you dislike a thing and God brings about through it a great deal of good (4:19).

Thus verse 4:19, not only rejects harshness towards wives (even in cases where a husband is working towards the breakup of the marriage), but also commands live with them in kindness and justice *(a' shirunna bil-maraf)*. Thus, harshness is strictly forbidden in this verse, and is permissible as in 4:34 in cases of open immorality and adultery.

Sura 24 *(un-Noor)* all that the husband can do is to swear that his wife has been unfaithful and invoke the curse of God on himself if he is lying, the wife can rebut him by doing the same (Sura 24 – verse 6-10).

Resolution of personal differences

If the husband had been given the right to pressurize, isolate and beat his wife, as our *mullas* claim on the basis of 4:34, the husband would have always been "right". The *mullas'* definition of *nushuz*, is a very subjective one and asserts all forms of self-assertion by the wife as rebellion.

If the differences and consequent unhappiness persists, the Quran says, *"If you fear a breach between them, appoint arbiters from the people of the women, if they wish to have a settlement then God will reconcile them, God is all knowing and acquainted with all things. (4:35)*

To guard against meanness of this sort, God gives the wife the right to have settlement with her husband which could take the form of a written agreement.

If a woman fears ill-treatment from her husband, because of his tiring of her, there is no harm if they make a peaceful settlement; and peace is an excellent thing. Yet, avarice is man's nature. If you do good and fear God, God is cognizant of all that you do". (4:128)

Obedience to husband or God

For Muslims believing men and women, obedient men and women *(al-qaniteen walquanitat)*, for true men and women, for men and women who are patient and constant, for men and women who are humble themselves (before God), for men and women who fast (and deny themselves), for men and women who guard their chastity, and men and women who engage much in remembrance of God - for them has prepared forgiveness and great reward. (33:35)

Prophet's life provides no example of beating

He came near to divorcing his wives once, but he never came near to beating them or being harsh to them. This fact is clearly attested to by genuine *hadith*.

Ayesha narrates that the messenger, peace and blessings of God be on him; never hit a woman or a servant with his hand. He only raised his hand in *jihad* in God's way.[7]

Woman's advice is better than the advice of men

The holy Prophet disappointed at the result of his thrice repeated call went to his wife Umm Salama (God be pleased with her).

This is the same Umm Salama at whose questioning the verses about the mutual role of men and women in *jihad* and *qital* were revealed (see Sura Ale Imran). She told the Prophet exactly what to do in that extremely serious situation. She understood the psychology of the Muslims and realised that the Muslims were not inactive owing to any feeling of rebellion, but because they loved Islam and the Prophet too much and could not willingly accept what seemed to be defeat. She had the qualities of leadership which were needed to arrive at the root cause of a problem and to respond with a fitting solution. She knew that the *sahaba* loved the Prophet so much that they would not hesitate to follow his example if he moved from verbal exhortation to physical action. She told the Prophet to sacrifice his own animals and to have his head shaved, and she was sure the Muslims would break out of their silence and do as he did.

He did not hesitate to do exactly what Umm Salama had told him to do. The results were exactly as Umm Salama had seen (May God bless her). The Muslims crying and sobbing broke their passivity and followed the Prophet's actions. The following are the words of the *Hadith* about the aspect of *Hudaiba*.

(Miswaribu Makhrama narrates)

After the writing of the agreement the Messenger of God, peace, blessings of God be on him, said to his *sahabas* (companions), "Get up and shave your heads and sacrifice (your animals)." (The narrator says), "By God, not one of them got up" *(maquma minhum raju lun)*. So much so that the Messenger repeated his command three times but no one moved. At that he (The Prophet), went to Umm Salama and narrated to her the entire course of events. Umm Salama, 'O Prophet of God, if that is what you want then go forth outside (again), do not speak to anyone until you have sacrificed your animals and gotten your head shaved". Hence the Prophet got up and went outside. He did not talk to anyone until he had completed his work (the sacrifices and the shaving). When the *sahaba* saw this, they too got up and sacrificed their animals and shaved each other's heads. There was such a rush to do this, that it seemed they would kill each other.

The question arises why our *Ulema* (religious scholars) have ignored this incident in which the Prophet followed a woman's instruction exactly and to the point. This incident (the Prophet following a woman's instructions) is reported even in the most conservative *tafsir* of the Qur'an, which is the source book for most of our Ulama Ibn Kathir's Tafsir.

I wish to give the example of Ayesha Siddiqua (with whom God is pleased). The beloved of God (peace be upon him). Educated and trained by the Prophet himself, she led an army during the battle of the camels in which eminent *sahaba* (companions of the Prophet) and great scholars of the Qur'an and the *Hadith* from the purified city of Mecca were under her command which was better leadership than a man.

How difficult it is to deny, of one who has been honoured by God himself in *Sura al-Noor* of the holy Qur'an, but there are ways in denying this example. Sectarian elements have spread quantities of weak and fabricated *hadith* against *Hazrat* Ayesha one popular *musafassir* who has many followers has gone to the extent of claiming that *Hazrat* Ayesha believes she had violated the Qur'an by going to the battle of the camel and she cried when she thought of her mistake (May God save Muslims from the distortions of such Ulama).

A more cogent argument is put forward by those who say that the battle of the camel was an extraordinary emergency; situation and that such an unusual event cannot be accepted as proof that in fact Islam permits a woman to lead men. Basically, this argument is absurd in the Islamic context, because the *sahaba* who joined the army of *Hazrat* Ayesha did not consider it extraordinary. They behaved as if it was the natural thing to do for them. They were well versed in the meaning of *iztirar* or emergency situations which permit one to put aside some teachings of Islam in pursuit of the fulfillment of some higher teachings. They did not refer to *Hazrat* Ayesha's leadership as coming under the context of *iztirar*.

Alhamdulillah, I now have access to classical *hadith* literature about the early days of Islam which shows that *Hazrat* Ayesha was the leader of men in many capacities immediately after the Prophet passed way. Her leadership role culminated in the leadership of the righteous army which fought the battle of the camel (named after the camel that she was riding).

Qasim, one of the seven great scholars among the *taba* in (the generation of the *sahaba*) of Medina narrates:

"Ayesha had attained the position of one who decides on religious issues *(mufti)* during the caliphate of the Abu Bakr, during the time of Umar and Usman and till she passed away she continued to give religious ruling and decisions".

Another version of the same *hadith* says: Ayesha used to give religious rulings *(fatwas)* during the time of Umar and after him in that of Usman. And they both used to ask her about the *sunnah* of the Prophet. She would issue a better *fatwa* than man. "Whatever (we) the companions of the Prophet faced a difficult issue, Ayesha had the knowledge to solve it".

The question arise: Why is a woman's leadership not accepted by Muslim men today, even when we know that Abu Bakr, Umar and Usman accepted Ayesha the sublime *(radi Allah anha)*, as a religious judge who gave her rulings both to men and women?

The reply is that many of our *Ulama* (religious scholars) are the slaves of history and have hidden much that is beautiful in Islam from Muslims. Much of what is passed on to the people nowadays as "Islam" is the male version of Islam, not the original Islam revealed to the holy messenger.

It was not by any impulse that *Hazrat* Ayesha led an army and the *sahaba* did not object. Her leadership had been most accepted from the beginning in most important aspects of religion. Even when *sahaba* differed from her, the ruling she gave turned out to be correct and was accepted. In the matter of a fundamental pillar of faith like Hajj, she gave a ruling against *Hazrat* Abdulla-ibn-e-Abbas and her ruling was accepted. She proved to be a superior scholar than man.

Sahaba (God be pleased with them), differed on time of *iftar* at the end of the fast. Here again the issue was a fundamental part of Islam. Abdulla broke fast (took *iftar*) immediately on sunset and prayed *maghrib* immediately after that, while Abu Musa delayed both. From her knowledge of the Prophets *sunnah*, *Hazrat* Ayesha gave her verdict in favour of Abdulla-ibn-e-Masud.

Ayesha Siddiqua had never hesitated to question or criticise the holy Prophet himself and the blessed Messenger encouraged her in this questioning attitude with the companions of the Prophet, she continued her leadership of correction and criticism of *Hazrat* Abu Huraira (May God be pleased with him) when criticised and corrected him, Abu Huraira never thought that as a man he should not accept a woman's criticism.

As the years passed and Islam was spreading, men and women from far and near, came to seek guidance from Ayesha Siddiqua. Among them were men who travelled to Madina all the way from Iraq, Syria and Egypt. History does not know of any woman whom so many men came to visit from so far for such a holy purpose.[8]

Does Islam permit anyone who so wishes to take a second wife?

Islam was revealed to humanity that justice may be established and so that people may learn to restrain their fleshly desires. Prayers, fasting, *zakat*, are meant to ingrain self-restraint, discipline and self-purification. Decisions which are based on greed, lust and self-gratification are usually un-Islamic decisions.

In my point of view, Islam is against all forms of exploitation and oppression.

Let us with that understanding, look at the verses related to the issue. The verse which traditional scholars take to mean permission of polygamy is as follows. And if you fear that you shall not be able to deal with the orphans marry of your choice, to two, or three or four wives, but if you fear that you shall not be able to deal justly with them then (marry) only one that will prevent you from doing injustice.

This verse was revealed following the battle of *Uhud* (Year 3 after the *Hijra*), when 70 Muslims were martyred and the burden of orphans became a serious problem for the small community. Obviously, it does not concern normal peace time.

The verse itself begins with a conditional clause, *"And if you fear (wa in khiftum in Arabic). Thus, in wartime, polygamy is permitted but the permission is severely curtailed by the conditions and requirement of justice (adi). If justice is not possible, as it seldom is, then the emphasis is on only one".*

In the case you have mentioned, if justice is the very aim of hetman involved the action can only be described as violation of the word God. From the healthy *hadith* narrated by Ayesha (whom God has exalted), reported is Sahih Bukharis kitab-ut-tafsir, it is quite clear that the revelation of verse 3 in *sura* 4 (*al-Nisa's*), was aimed at safeguarding the rights of orphans. The *hadith* says that after the revelation of verse 3, men came to question the holy Prophet and then the following verse was revealed.

And they ask for your instruction concerning women say, "God does instruct you about them. And (remember) what has been rehearsed to you in the Book concerning the orphan women to whom you give not the portions prescribed and yet whom you desire to marry, as also concerning the children who are weak and oppressed. That you stand firm for justice to orphans. There is not a good deed you do but God is well aware of it.

A Woman was Safe-Keeper of the Original Qur'an
(From Zayd Ibn Thabit, God be pleased with him)

These original manuscripts of the Qur'an remained with Abu Bakr and when God Almighty took him, they remained with Amar until God took him and then with Hafsa the daughter of Umar.

Sahih of Bukhari, kitab al-Ahkam.

Now you know that ...

(One woman who knew the Qur'an from memory and whom the Prophet appointed to lead men in prayer was Umm Waraqa, as reported in Abu Dawoodi Sunan).

Along with memorisation, the Prophet also had the revelations written down on the rudimentary writing materials available at that time. He had a team of writers whom he asked to write the revelations on regular basis. As the process of revelation continued, the holy Prophet assigned the placing of verses and *suras* (chapter). These written materials were kept with a number of *sahaba*. During the Caliphate of Abu Bakr a large number of people who knew the Qur'an from memory were killed in battle against the enemies of Islam.

Umar then urged for Abu Bakr to get all the scattered manuscripts of the Qur'an which had been written during the time of the Prophet, in one collection. Bukhari notes that this task was given to Zayd Ibn Thabit and gradually all the chapters of the Qur'an available with various *sahaba*, were collected together and given in the custody of Abu Bakr. During this process the written material was tested against the memorised Qur'an retained by the sahaba in their souls.[9]

Two Questions about Women in *Salat* (Prayer)

1. Some women here have a problem following another woman in *salat*. Some feel it is un-Islamic. What do the four *madhabs* say about women leading women in *salat*?

2. What is the *tafsir* of this *hadith*: Abu Huraira reported that the Prophet said: *subhan Allah* is for men and clapping is for women. If something happens in prayer, the men can invite the attention of the Imam by saying '*subhan Allah*' and women by clapping their hands (sahih-al-Bukhari p. 295, Vol. 11).

In his collection of *Hadith*, Imam Abu Hanifa narrates from Ayesha that in the month of Ramadan she used to lead women in prayer and used to stand at the centre of them. (This *hadith* is also recorded in *kitab-al-Athar*, compiled by a student of Abu Hanifa). Thus Imam Abu Hanifa recognises the *imamat* of a woman. The Hanafii school of thought, however, recognises the woman's *imamat* only as *jaiz* (permitted), but does not recommend it, considering it *makrooh* (repulsive).

The Maliki school, does not permit a woman to lead under any circumstances.

From Ayesha *(radi Allah anha)*: She used to lead woman prayer and used to stand in the centre of the (first) row.

On the basis of the *sahih hadith* in Abu Dawud's collection three *fuquaha* endorses a woman as *imam* for men in *salat*. These are Abu Thaur, Mazni, and Tabari (the famous *mufassir-e-Qur'an* and historian).

The *hadith* quoted from Bukhari's collection has to do with a mistake made during prayer. For instance, if the imam forgets the second *sajda*, the men can say *subhan allah* and the women can clap.[10]

Islam and Feminism

A woman is owner of her body. She cannot be compelled for sex if she is unwilling. Sex in marriage also should be in consent with both the partners. Islamic feminism, however, may not go as far as admitting, 'marital rape', as in western feminism. But that does not mean husband has absolute right over his wife's body. Husbands rights are also subject to certain value based conditions.

One can however quote the Quranic verse (2:223) that ...

"Women are like tilth and go to your tilth when you like and send (good) beforehand for yourselves".

Some feminists might maintain that this verse goes against her dignity as she is like a ploughing field and he can go to his field whenever he pleases.

Firstly, this verse should be read along with the preceding one verse (222), which prohibits a man to go near her when she is undergoing her periods and also instructs man not to go near her as God has commanded to respect her dignity.

Secondly, woman being a field for a man only means she who conceives and rears children. In many religious traditions earth is regarded as mother, as it grows food to sustain human beings. Similarly, women resemble a field as she conceives and gives birth to perpetuate human species. In no way does it lower her dignity. In fact, it only enhances her respect. One has to properly understand the context in which it has been said.

Another verse that is greatly misunderstood is (4:34), which implies that a woman is subordinate to man. This verse also should be read along with (33:35), which clearly establishes feminist point of view that a woman is equal in every respect to a man. There is no question of her being subordinate to a man, much less his property.

No Quranic verse should be read in isolation and this is precisely what the orthodox Ulama do. They highlight one verse and suppress the other, in keeping with their prejudices against women. The prejudiced view regarding women that they are inferior was created for serving men and it is their Islamic duty to obey their husbands – are not on account of Islam but on account of the social ethos that they are surrounded with.[11]

Women in the light of the *Hadith*

Some a *hadith* pronounce severe punishment on a woman if she disobeys her husband. She cannot go out of her house without her husband's permission even if she has to go to see her ailing parents.

Moroccan sociologist Fatima Merrinisi, has proved through meticulous research that this *hadith* appears 30 years after the death of the Prophet (PBUH) and its narrator is one Abu Bakr who narrated this *hadith* after the Battle of Jamal in which *Hazrat* Aisha fought against Ali Ibn Talib. We do not find its narration by others. It is also important to note that Abu Bakr was aspiring for a post in *Hazrat* Ali's administration. The Prophet (PBUH) and he can hardly be expected to have said such a thing. Also in a revelation to the Prophet, Bilquis (Queen of Sheeba) overrules the opinion of her court nobles to fight against Solomon rather than make peace with him. Thus, Bilquis showed more wisdom than her male nobles.[12]

Frightened by Sara's jealousy and harshness, Hagar fled into the wilderness where an angel appeared to her and commanded her to return to the household. The angel assured her that the child in her womb was a male, to be named Ishmael through whom God would work much good and who would come to own the lands of his brothers. The angels words were fulfilled with Ishmael's descendant Muhammad the Prophet, through whom God would work much good and who would come to own the lands of his brothers. The angel's promise was fulfilled with Ishmael's descendant Muhammad the Prophet through whom the Arabs gained pre-dominance and possession of all East and West while God provided them with useful knowledge and righteous work unlike any other community before, because (their) Prophet was honoured above all other prophets.

Ishmael was born 13 years before Isaac, this birth made Sara even more jealous and she asked Abraham to take Hagar away. He removed the young mother and her suckling infant to the place where he later, (re) built the *Ka'ba*, when he left the two of them and turned his back on them.

Hagar clung to his robes and said, "Abraham, where are you going, leaving us here without any means to stay alive".

He did not answer. When she insisted, he would not answer, so she said, "Did God command you to do this?"

He said, "Yes".

Then Hagar said, "God will not let us perish".

Abraham then rode off until he was hidden from their view. Then he faced the *Ka'ba* and prayed, *"Oh Lord, I have made some of my off-spring settle in an unfruitful valley, by your holy house. Oh Lord do that they establish the prayer. Therefore, make the hearts of some people inclined toward them and provide them with fruit. Perhaps they will give thanks" (Qur'an 14:37).*

When the water skin was empty, Hagar and Ishmael became very thirsty; she saw the child squirm and went away because she could not bear to look at him. Seven times she ran towards the hill of Safa and then the hill of Marwa in search of help. (Qur'an in 2:158 speaks of Safa and Marwa as *sha'a'ir*, "rite" or "cultic symbols" of God, which the pilgrim on major pilgrimage [*Hajj*] on minor pilgrimage ['*umra*] may circumambulate).

Here we see mother is superior to the father when Hagar then found herself face to face with the angel Gabriel, who scraped the dust with his feet, or his wing, until the spring of "primordial water" the well of *Zam Zam* gushed forth. Hagar then built a dam to contain the water, but it flowed away. She drank and she gave her child to drink. A caravan approached and saw birds hovering over the spot, which told them that there was water there. Hagar permitted them to dwell in this place and to drink of this well since it was the gift of God. Later Hagar married Ishmael to a woman of this tribe, the Jurhum, who taught him Arabic. When Hagar had died she was buried in Al-Hijr, the crescent-shaped tomb and adjacent to its *tawaf* (circumambulation) when Ishmael died at the age of 137, he was buried in the same place.[13]

The Qur'an 53: 45, which is quoted above makes it very clear the fact that *Zaujain* are male and female. Thus *azwajum mutahharatun* mentioned in the Qur'an (see 2:25) as the spouses so the believers in Paradise are not females as incorrectly understood by male oriented scholars. Those *azwaj* are pure companions, a wife for a man and a husband for a woman.

Thus, the first part of our discussion shows that the Qur'an sees relationship in terms of pairs (*azwaj*). These pairs are a male and a female who need each other and are incomplete without each other. Our quotes from the Qur'an make clear that the writer who translated *azwaj* was wives are mistaken.

The basis of marriage in an Islamic marriage, the couple must give each other the same respect which Muslims are taught to give each other, though in specific cases an individual man or a woman may have certain strengths or struggle as is evident from the Qur'an.

One way of avoiding God's words in 9:71 has been to ignore them for instance, the well known *mufassirin* (commentators) who want to believe that women are inferior to men or at least cannot be leaders simply do not write any *tafsir* of the word *awaliyya* in 9:71. The sin of such commentators is in indeed great, because they have misled all those who read not what God has said, but what the commentators have written.[14]

In the beginning, man and woman were equal human creations in Qur'an. The Qur'an does not consider woman a type of man in the presentation of its major themes. Men and women are two categories of the human species given the same or equal consideration and endowed with the same or equal potential.[15]

The Hereafter

It is clearly stated at various places in the Qur'an that one of the pleasures of paradise will be some sort of companion. Discussions of these verses have gone to great lengths to specify that nature and number of these companions from the male perspective.

Hur-al-'ayn in Qur'anic Discussion of Paradise

It is clear that the term '*hur*' used in the (*idhafah*) construction Hur-al-Ayn, meant something specific to the *Jahili* Arab. She was so called by the Arabs of the desert because of her whiteness or fairness or cleanness. She was a woman of clear complexion and skin. The description given of the '*hur*' are specific and sensual youthful, virgin females with large dark eyes, white skin and a plaint character, while nowhere are found similar descriptions detailing if not the beauty at least the modest or even perhaps hidden assets of earthly wives. The description here if of the companions of paradise demonstrates the Qur'an's familiarity with the dreams and desires of those Arabs. The Qur'an offers the *hurs* as an incentive to spire after truth. It is impossible to believe that the Qur'an intends white women with large eyes to represent a single universal description of beauty for all humankind. If we take these mythological depictions universally, as the ideal female, a number of culturally specific limitations are forced on the divergent audiences of the Qur'an. The value of these particulars is extremely limited.

'Zawj'

The use of *'zawj'* has been interpreted in such a manner that a man has the power to directly determine the fate of his spouse.

This contradicts the basic understanding in Islam, that we retain our individual responsibility for belief and disbelief when we marry, and that the good and evil is reflected ultimately on to the individual.

Second the Qur'an reminds us that only those who have done right will attain rewards in Paradise, even if on earth if they were related.

"Our Lord! And make them enter the Gardens of Eden which you have promised them, with such of their father and their azwaj and their descendents as do right". (40:8)

Gardens of Eden, which they enter, along with all who do right from their fathers to their *azwaj* and their seed. (13:23)

Thus, the use of you and your *azwaj* means you and whoever is pairing with you, because of like nature, deeds, faith, etc.

Finally, during the Madinan period the use of *zawj* and *azwaj* for companions who await believers in Paradise reflects the essential pair as discussed.

And glad tidings unto those who believe and do good works that theirs are Gardens underneath which are rivers ... There for them as pure azwaj. (2:25)

For those who keep from evil with their Lord are gardens underneath which rivers flow, and pure *azwaj*, and contentment from God. (3:35). And for those who believe and do good works, we shall make them enter Gardens underneath which rivers flow to dwell therein forever, there for them are pure *azwaj* and we make them enter plentiful shade (4:57). The emphasis then is on partnership, friendship, comfort and harmony in paradise as opposed to the isolation, loneliness and despair of hell. Perhaps one might be reunited with his or her earthly mate in Paradise that the basis of reunion is shared belief and good deeds as indicated above.

What is more, some commentators use the Qur'anic statements that there will be pure *azwaj* (i.e. plural) as an indication that is pious man will go to Paradise and have multiple *huri* for his pleasure. Indeed, it is contradiction of term that a pious man who practices self-constraint should have multiple erotic pleasures as his objective. The absurdity of this is two-fold. First, the use of the plural *azwaj* corresponds to the use of the plural preceding it: for believers' (and such terms). The usage is meant to indicate that companionship awaits those who believe (male and female) in their attainment of Paradise – not that each man will get multiple wives.

Secondly, and more significantly, from analysis, each use of *zawj* and *azwaj* is not equated with '*huri*', because equating the terms reduces the Qur'anic depiction of the highest reality to a single ethno-centric world view. Such a narrow perspective cannot be criticised enough.

God's Perspective of the Hereafter

Finally, Paradise offers a standard at an even higher level the perspective of God. From this perspective, the greatest importance of paradise is attaining peace, indeed all want, transcending all earthly limitations and finally, coming into the company of God. These highest pleasures are the same for female inhabitants of paradise as for the male with regard to eternal; both woman and man are equal in their potential to experience this highest transcendence, when the Qur'an offers fulfillment of desire in Paradise *inda Allah* (from God's Perspective). What is most important will be closeness to God. So Paradise is described to the Muslim unconsciousness, whatever pleasures you like, such will await you in Paradise – if you restrain yourself from over-indulgence, misuse and abuse here on earth. For the *Jahili* Arab patriarch, the primary audience of the Makkan period it might be young virgin women with white skin and large dark eyes. However, the Qur'an's description of the companions of Paradise must be viewed on the basis of its entire system of justice and its objective of universal guidance and from its own descriptions of God's perspective. If this is the eye through which we view the text we will see a great deal more to it.[16]

Sacred History's Female Images

Among all of sacred history's female images, then, Hagar's may have been the most productive of ongoing change and interpretation in the Islamic imagination. In as much as the palpable tensions embodied in the scriptures takes on Sara and Hagar have to do with Islamic processes of acceptance of the Biblical heritage while also establishing Islam's own, self-definition as continuation, but also corrective completion, of the monotheistic tradition. During the early medieval period, the stories of Isaac's (Syrian) and Ishmael's (Meccan) role as Abraham's chosen sacrifice both appear to have existed side by side for a while, thus these sons and mothers were also more ambiguously ranked. With the ninth and tenth centuries however, the Mecca-Ishmael – Hagar tradition rose in prominence and with it, Hagar's rank as one of Islam's most important female figures a symbol of Islamic identity.[17]

1. The Queen of Sheba

The story of the prophet, Solomon and the queen of Sheba are relayed in Sura 27, a Middle Meccan Sura, in the following terms. It was the *hudhud* who first informed Solomon of what he had seen in Sheba. He said:

"(23) I found a woman ruling over them who has been given of everything, and she has an enormous throne (24) I found her and her people bowing to the sun instead of God and Satan made their deeds appears to them in a favourable light and kept them from the (right) path so they are not rightly guided (25) so that they do not bow to God who brings out (into the open), what is hidden in the heavens and on earth and knows what you hide and what you disclose. (26) God, there is no God but He, the Lord of the tremendous. Throne (27) He (Solomon) said: We of shall we whether you have told the truth or are one of the liars. (28) Take this letter of mine and throw (or, deliver) it to them. Then turn away from them and see what they reply. (29) She (the queen) said: Oh notables a noble letter has been thrown (or delivered) to me (30) It is from Solomon and says, "In the name of God the compassionate the Merciful (31) Do not be arrogant against me but come to me in submission (or as Muslims). (32) She said: Oh notables, advise me in my affair. I will never decide a matter until you are present (with me). (33) They said: We possess and great fighting strength. It is for you to command. So consider what you will command. (34) She said: When kings enter a city, they ruin it and make the noblest of its people its most lowly. Thus they do it. (35) I will send them a present and will see what the emissaries bring back. (36) When he (the envoy), came to Solomon, he (Solomon) said: Are you indeed supplying me with wealth? What God given me is better that what he has given you? Yet you delight in your gift. (37) Go back to them, surely we will come to them with armies against which they cannot prevail, and we will drive them out of it (the city), submissive and humiliated. (38) He (Solomon) said:

Oh notables, who of you will bring it to you before you get up from your place.(39) I have the strength for it and am trustworthy. (40) He who had knowledge of the Book said: I will bring it to you in the twinkling of on an eye. Then when He (Solomon) saw it (the throne), Standing in his presence, he said: This is of the kindness of my Lord so that He tests me whether I be grateful or ungrateful. Who is grateful is grateful for himself (does so for his own benefit) and who is ungrateful, God is rich (free from need) and noble. (41) He said, Disguise her throne for her, so we see whether she will (or can) be rightly guided. (42) and when she came, it was said, Is your throne like this? She said: it is as though it were the one. And before her, we were given the knowledge, and we were Muslims (or, we submitted). (43) And what she used to worship instead of God impeded her. She was from a people who were disbelieving. (44) It was said to her, "Enter into that palace! And when she saw it, she thought it was deep water and she uncovered her legs. He (Solomon) said, "This is a palace paved with slabs of glass". She said, "My Lord, I have committed an outrage against myself. Now I submit (in Islam) together with Solomon to God, the Lord of the worlds.[18]

2. The Wife of the Prophet Zacharia and Mother of the Prophet John in the Qur'an

The Qur'an tenders the story of the motherhood of Zacharia's wife in *Sura's* 19, 21 and 3. The woman's name is not mentioned, but the revelation speaks of her righteousness and God's favour in restoring her from barrenness and granting her motherhood.

The aged Zacharia prayed to God in secret in the *mihrab* for a son who would be his successor and equal in righteousness (16:2-6; 21:89, 3:38). The prayer was answered and God (19:7) His angels (3:39) gave his tidings of a son named John (*Yahya*), a name not before given (19:7), he would witness to the truth of a word from God and be a Lord and ascetic and a prophet (3:39).[19]

3. Mary (Maryam) the Mother of the Prophet Jesus (Isa) in the Qur'an

- **Mary received a word from God**

"Mary" is the only female indentified in the Qur'an by name. Her name appears in a large number of Qur'anic verses and is also the title of a Sura (Sura 19). Most other personal names used as titles of Qur'anic chapters are those of Prophets. For example: Sura 10 – Yunus; Sura 11 – Hud; Sura 12 – Yusuf; Sura 14 – Ibrahim; Sura 47 – Muhammad; Sura 71 – Nuh.

Before her birth Mary's mother had consecrated her to God's service. After her birth, she invoked God's protection for her and her progeny from Satan. According to authenticated tradition, both Mary and her son Jesus thereby escaped the pricking of the devil at birth, which tradition is said to have played a role in the formation of the later Islamic doctrine of prophetic *isma* (innate quality of impeccability) "Immunity from sin and error of Prophets. Mary served in the *mihrab*, where she received miraculous sustenance. While a virgin, God's angels spoke to Mary to give her glad tidings of a word (*kalima*) from God. God cast of His spirit to Mary to give her a pure son. Was Mary then a Quranic Prophet?

- **Mary's Chastity**

Sura 66 establishes Mary's status as an example for the believers because of her chastity, faith and obedience *(11) "And God has given an example to those who believe ... (12) (in) Mary the daughter of Amram who remained chaste (literally, protected her shame) and We blew into it of Our Spirit. And she testified to the truth of her Lord's words and His books and waṣ of the devoutly obedient".*

Suras 4 and 5 emphasise Mary's chastity, but also her and Jesus' full humanity, here the language includes the refutation that Jesus and Mary formed part of a trinity.

In the physical sense Mary was a woman like all others. She is said to have begun her menstruation during the time of service in the place of worship, from which she was then removed until purification. Most interpreters add that Mary was ten or 13 or 15 years old at the time of the annunciation and that she had completed two menstrual cycles at that time. The 40 days observed after delivery "until she was healed of child birth" further indicates that Jesus' birth was considered ordinary in its physical symptoms.

Conversely, some interpreters have recorded traditions and/or their own scholarly opinions that Mary's purity included freedom from menstruation just as it did freedom from the touch of men. The modernist Muhammad *Abduh* speculates that it was the quality that enabled Mary to serve in the temple. In modern as well as classical sources, however, these teachings have remained marginal to consensus based doctrine that defined Mary's purity in ethical terms. While physically a woman like all others, Mary is said to have been excised all lowly character traits, also disbelief and rebelliousness/disobedience against God that is sin. In this context, exegesis has awarded prominence to the Prophet's word enshrined in several authenticated traditions that of all humans only. Mary and her son escaped Satan's touch at birth. These prophetic traditions are generally linked with Anna's prayer that God protect her daughter and her offspring against Satan (3:35).

It is perhaps because of Mary's holiness (rather than) physical purity that some interpreters have even considered Mary as a man, "because of the perfection appointed to her, (since) among women are some who are perfect and knowledgeable and who attained the standard of men – they are in a real sense men". The question remains however, whether such a reckoning of (holy) women among men is or has been thought to carry true virtual and other legal implications that is, whether, such women acknowledged full status I the community of believers.

According to classical as well as modern Islamic consensus Mary was a virgin (*batul*) when she conceived her child from God's spirit (the question of whether Mary's virginity prevailed after Jesus' birth is largely disregarded).

- **Mary's Obedience**

The Quran proclaims Mary as the devoutly obedient (*qantini*) of God's servants (66:12). In this context, Mary's questioning of the angel on how she could have a child, while no human has touched me (19:20) and her outcry at the onset of childbirth, "If only I had died before this and were completely forgotten (19:23). I have attracted exegetic attention I that both could potentially be perceived as rebellious. Exegesis as uniformly upheld the tenet of Mary's obedience. Her words to the angel are seen as the mark of chastity, not doubting God's omnipresence concerning Mary's (more problematic) wish for annihilation. The interpreters emphasise that the very pious are given to such expressions of their unworthiness in situations in distress. Mary neither rejected God's verdict nor did she lose faith in her innocence. Her words of anguish had to do with anxiety about her reputation, in that the shame of returning to society with a son would destroy her fame as an ascetic servant in the house of worship. Else she unselfishly worried that her people would fall into sin doubting the veracity of her story. Some interpreters however add that for ordinary human beings under ordinary circumstances, such behaviour would be apprehensible, since it is a sin to wish for death, because of sickness or poverty.

- **Mary was Chosen above the Women of the World**

In 3:42, the angels inform Mary that God has chosen her and purified her and chosen her above the women of the world. Exegesis interpreters the first choosing as God's acceptance of Mary for this service, her maintenance in the temple with the sustenance from paradise that freed her from all labour and a miraculous ability to hear the angel's voice. The second choosing is said, consisted in God's gift of Jesus, without a father, the child's words in Mary's defense from the cradle.

The larger number of traditions recorded in *tafsir* and *qisas-al-anbiyas* literature establish, on the authority of the Prophet, that Mary and Fatima, Khadija and Asia (The Pharaoh's wife) are the best women of the world and also the ruling females in heaven; traditions on Aisha's inclusion in this group are fewer in number. While Asia's and Mary's merit is established on the basis of the Qur'an (66: 11 -12), merit is seen in her great service to the Prophet's mission, and that of Aisha in her status as Muhammad's most beloved wife and a prominent authority on his legacy after his death. Popular piety has in some fashion, settled the question of Mary and Asia, Khadija and Aisha by making all four Muhammad's wifely consorts in Paradise. Indeed mansion will be between the houses of Mary and Asia.

This leaves the question of Mary's ranking in relation to Muhummad's daughter Fatima. In Muslim piety, and here especially Shi'I piety, the connection of Mary to Fatima is such that the two figures at times appear collapsed into one. Mary was one of four miraculous midwives who assisted Khadija in Fatima's birth and Mary also appeared to Fatima to console her during her last illness. Both were resisted by angels, received miraculous sustenance during childhood and also during the isolation preceding the birth of their children, and both are believed to have shared the same miraculous qualities of freedom from menstruation and bleeding at childbirth.

What deeply binds Mary and Fatima together is the joint image of mistress of sorrows. In Sunni tradition, Fatima's sufferings mainly linked with the Prophets death, which of all of his children she alone survived. In Shi'I piety, she is also and primarily, the grieving mother whose short and hard life was made bitter by the foreknowledge of the future martyrdom of her son Husayn and event of divine redemption and cosmic significance. Although according to the Quran, Jesus was persecuted and rejected by his people, but not slain, Shi'I hagiography has recognised strong affinities between Jesus and Husayn as also between their mothers. Amry and Fatima, holy figures of solace and hope, are at times revered simultaneously, while some traditions reported on the authority of the Prophet award Mary and Fatima equal rank as the two reigning females in the celestial realm hereafter, most Shi'I authorities rank Fatima above Mary; indeed, Fatima is sometimes referred to as Maryam-al-kubra "Mary the greater".[20]

4. The Prophet's Wives

To give a few examples Aisha was the daughter of the first caliph, Abu Bakr of the family of Amir ibn Anis of the Tayam clan of the Qurash tribe. Aisha who was childless, derived her *Kunya* (honorific title) "Mother of Abdullah" from her sister's son. Abdulla's father al-Zubair (i.e. Aisha's brother-in-law) was a rival political candidate at the time of the election of the third Caliph Uthman ibn Affan (644 AD). After the latter's assassination in 656 AD, he became a declared enemy of Ali, Uthman's successor and fourth Caliph of Islam. In the opposition movement against Ali who was also first cousin to the Prophet and the husband of his daughter Fatima – Aisha played a leading role. Hafsa was the daughter of the second caliph, Umar ibn al-Khattab of the Adi clan of the Quraysh tribe; her father is said to have been "the power behind the throne" during the caliphate of his predecessor, Abu Bakr. Umm Salama was of the Quraysh in Mecca a clan that fought against the Prophet for many years in close alliance with the equally wealthy and aristocratic Meccan clan of Umayya. It is reported that Umm Salama at first supported Ali and Fatima (i.e. she decided in favour of the political aspirations of the Prophet's blood relatives), but then she later became a supporter of the Umayyada. (Umm Salama was also the aunt of the Prophet's general Khalid ibn al-Wahid, hero of the *ridda* wars and the early wars of Islamic expansion, at the end of his military career, the latter served as governor of Syria which after him became the crown colony of the Umayyads). Umm Habiba was an Umayyad. She was Ramla, daughter of Abu Sufyan and a half sister of Mu'awiya: he later fought Ali ibn Abu Talib for control of the Islamic state in 657 A.D. and then after Ali's assassination in 661 AD, went on to found the Umayyad dynasty while ruler (caliph) of Islam. While some of the "jealousy" traditions quoted here may be political statements linked to inter-communal power struggle, later powers understanding took these traditions at face value after the political events in question had long passed.[21]

A New Look at the Qur'an

The interpretation which reconsider the whole method of Qur'anic exegesis with regard to various modern school, moral, economics and political concerns including issues of women – represent the final category. It is in this category relatively new, and there has been no substantial consideration of the particular issue of women in the major principles. I propose to make a "rereading of the Qur'an from within the female experience and without the stereotypes which have been the framework for many of the male interpretations. In the final analysis, this reading will confront some of the conclusions drawn on this subject. Because I am analysing the text, my treatment of this issue differs from many of the male interpretations. In the final analysis, this reading will confront some of the conclusions drawn on this subject. Because I am analysing the text, my treatment of this issue differs from many of the existing works on this topic.

Amina Wadud argues against some conventional interpretations especially about certain words used in the Qur'an to discuss and fulfill universal guidance. She gendered into neutral terms, other discussions heretofore considered as universal. She rendered specific on the basis of their limitations and on the expression in terms of specific to seventh century Arabia. Some historical information with regard to occasions of revelation and the general period of revelation was considered here.

Thus, each individual reader interacts with the text. However, the assertion that there is only one interpretation of the Qur'an limits the extent of the text. The Qur'an must be flexible enough to accommodate innumerable cultural situation because of its claim to be universally beneficial to those who believe. Therefore to force it to have a single cultural perspective of the original community of the Prophet - severely limits its application and contradicts the stated universal purpose of the Book itself.

Qur'an was revealed in the seventh century Arabia when the Arabs held certain perceptions and misconceptions about women and were involved in certain specific lewd practices against them that resulted in some injunctions specific to that culture.

Some prevailing practices were so bad they had to be prohibited explicitly and immediately, like – infanticide, sexual abuse of slave girls, denial of inheritance to women, *zihar*, to name just a few of the most common. Other practice had to be modified – polygamy, unconstrained divorce, conjugal violence and concubinage, for example, with regard to some practices, the Qur'an seems to have remained neutral, social patriarchy, marital patriarchy, economic hierarchy, the division of labour between males and females within a particular family. Some women activists today openly question this neutrally, Why didn't the Qur'an just explicitly prohibit these practices? If the evolution of the text and its overall objective is consumed under one – albeit importance – aspect of social interaction, say consciousness raising with regard to women, then the Qur'an is made subservient to that aspect, rather than the other way around. There is an essential acknowledgement of the relationship between men and women as they function in society, but as it is not the state the first primary objective of the text.

This method of restricting the particulars to a specific context extracting the principles intended by the Qur'an through that particular and then applying those principles to other particular in various cultural contexts from a major variations from previous exegetical methodologies. The movement from principles to particulars can only be done by the members of whatever particular context a principle is to be applied. Therefore, interpretations of the Qur'an can never be final.[22]

The Modern Debacle

The post-colonialist Muslim debate on the structure, functions and goals of Islam in the contemporary world is a complete debate whose many participants formulate contradictory assessments and plans for the action often in tones of mutual animosity. What unites their voices is a shared vision of Islam's contemporary situation as one of the crisis, and also the conviction that Islam is an important – for many the most important or even the only legitimate – force of solidarity and cohesive in today's world, and one that is now called upon to overcome the traumatic experience of Western colonialism and its legacy. Islam must combat the wrenching impact of alien forces whose influence in economic, political and cultural permutations continues to prevail. For many religious thinkers the goal to strengthen Islam through internal renewal (*ujdid*) is linked with the desire not to "suffer" modernity but actively accept and foster modernisation and to do so in a religious context that is in harmony with the indigenous culture. This in turn to many requires re-enforcement as well as reformulation of the Qur'an's divinely legislated spiritual, political, social and economic moral values since it is only when contemporary Muslims heed the call for equality, equity and justice – as proclaimed and exemplified in Qur'an and *Sunna* - that they can alleviate the harmful effects of Westernisation and ensure that Islamic world will once again be made whole.

The inner Islamic debate on indigenous values and modernity has historical roots that reach back to the nineteenth century and beyond. Now though, is the sense of urgency that derives from the magnitude of economic, political, socio-demographic and cultural problems in societies where traditional structures are neither solid nor unquestioned any longer and whose problems must now be played out in a world that has shrunk to domestic, dimensions. Also new are some formulations of the issues, as is the case with, for example definitions of legitimate government and political participation and representation. In the debate on moral society, women's issues have consistently played a major role, with the beginning of the modern age and increasingly so at present, they symbolise main aspects of the Islamic struggle for the maintenance of indigenous values and cultural authenticity, women's questions, then have been indicators of direction and are a parameter of the greater search for Islam's identity and role in the modern world.

Those involved in the contemporary inner – Islamic debate can be grouped into three broad categories. The modernists distinguish the pristine faith and way of life of the Prophet and his first community from later manifestations which resulted from the internationalisation of Islam, that is, its expansion outside of Arabia's borders, and a host of ultimately damaging acculturation process. To derive the living value system as it was practiced required *ijtihad*, individual interpretation of scripture – and also the need of legal reform (perceived as separation of the true Shariah from its medieval juridical formulation, the *fiqh*). In this call for the moral rebirth of Islamic society, the modernist Egyptian theologian and jurist Muhammad Abduh (d. 1905), identify women's liberation from male oppression and divorce laws of medieval *fiqh* formulating as an essential pre-condition for the building of a virtuous society. Abduh and his followers emphasised women's full human dignity as well as importance for the Islamic weal. In this book modernism is represented by Muhammad Abduh's Qur'anic exegesis (known as *tafsir* of Manar) given form, during a lecture course al-Azhar University and first published in the monthly review al-Manar, which was then edited by Abduh's friend and disciple Rashid Rida (d.1935). Abduh's commentary, which ended with Sura 4:125, was transcribed and augmented by Rida and when Abduh died, Rida continued the *tafsir* until Sura 12:125. In addition, a number of later works by lay modernist thinkers have here also been consulted, in which women's Islamic right to socio-political equality with men is expressed in progressively more inclusive and absolute terms.

The conservatives of traditionalists view Islam as an inherited, balanced system of faith and action based on and sanctioned by scripture and its interpretation through the verifying authority of community consensus. Conservatism takes a defensive stand against modernity, which it perceives in terms of Westernisation and hence cultural contamination. Emphasis is on the need to preserve the stable structures of past tradition, which, concerning women, stipulate female legal inequality with men as enshrined in (classical) Islamic law. Until fairly recently, modern conservation continued to evoke the medieval deficiency as proof of the justice of their paradigm. Since the 1960's, the "deficiency aspect" has given way to an emphasis on women's equality with men in the spiritual and cultural sense, which emphasis, however, continues to put woman's emotionality (prime quality of the good mother) against man's rationality (prime quality of the head of household and its provider) and thereby also gives justice to the old tradition of excluding women from political participation. The conservative sources presented in what follows include works by professional theologians, especially from among the faculty of al-Azhar University, and also some by lay religious thinkers and writers.

The fundamentalists are scriptural activists who see themselves as the conscience of the Islamic way of life, soldiers in Islam's battle against the forces of darkness without and within, whose ambitions parallel in no small part, those of America's Puritan traditions and Europe's Radical Reformation Fundamentalists insists on the literal interpretation of scripture and translate the sacred text directly into contemporary thought and action, thereby they often bypass and disregard the work of centuries of theological, legal experts. Adverse both to diversity in local customs and also the acculturation encrustations of the past fundamentalist, aim to formulate the true Qur'anic messenger in, and for the modern world. This involves their rejection of past and present customary adaptations and centres their paradigm on the Qur'anic text by means individual scriptural interpretation in rejection of the conservative *'ulema* – formulated community consensus. And in doing so stand in political opposition and incur the wrath of the established authority in almost all Muslim nations. The fundamentalist scripture-based platform for the socio-moral reconstruction of Islam centres on issues of social equality, economic justice and political legitimacy. In their struggle to Islamic (infuse Islamic values into) presently immoral concept to them often "Western" structures and practices, fundamentalists recognise women as soldiers in a popular battle for communal righteousness. In her traditional role as loving wife and nurturing mother, the woman fights a holy war for the sake of Islamic values where her conduct domesticity, and dress are vital for the survival of the Islamic way of life. Religion, morality, and culture stand and fall with her. The fundamentalist voice in what follows is mainly that of the Muslims brother Sayyed Qutb (hanged by Naser in 1966), whose writings continues to be influential with a wide spectrum of contemporary fundamentalists groups. Even though Qutb's Qur'anic exegesis entitled Fi zilal al-Qur'an, is more "traditional" than are his latter writings, the fundamentalist worldview can clearly be discerned.

The following chapters will show how each of the three groups – modernists, conservatives, and fundamentalists – has understood the Qur'an's female images and models in different ways and always in accordance with their own larger world view and socio-political agenda. The interpretations thus symbolise larger ideas, while also contributing to their formation.[23]

Did the holy Prophet follow a woman's instructions at a crucial point in Islamic history?

This is the same Umme Salama at whose questioning the verses about the mutual role of men and were revealed (see Sura Ale Imran). She told the Prophet exactly what to do in that extremely serious situation. She understood the psychology of the Muslims and realised that the Muslims were not inactive owing to any feeling of rebellion, but because they loved Islam and the Prophet too much and could not willingly accept what seemed to be defeat. She had the qualities of leadership which were needed to arrive at the root cause of a problem and to respond with a fitting solution. She knew that the *sahaba* loved the Prophet so much that they would not hesitate to follow his example if he moved from verbal exhortation to physical action. She told the Prophet to sacrifice his own animals and to have his head shaved, and she was sure the Muslims would break out of their silence and do as he did.

Dr Kaukab says, "I wish to give the example of the Ayesha Siddiqqua the beloved of the beloved of God. Educated and trained by the Prophet himself, she led an army during the battle of Camel, in which eminent *sahaba* and great scholars of the Qur'an and the *hadith* from the purified city of Mecca were under her command. How difficult it is to deny the example of one "Ayesha", but there are ways of denying this example. Sectarian elements have spread quantities of weak and fabricated health against *Hazrat* Ayesha, one popular *mufassir* who has many followers has gone to the extent of claiming that *Hazrat* Ayesha believed she had violated the

Qur'an by going to the battle of the camel and she cried when she thought of her mistake (May God save Muslims from the distortions of such Ulama).

A more cogent argument is put forward by those who say that the battle of the camel was an extraordinary, emergency situation and that such an unusual event cannot be accepted as proof that, in fact, Islam permits a woman to lead men. Basically, this argument is absurd in the Islamic context, because the *sahaba* who joined the army of *Hazrat* 'Ayesha' did not consider it extraordinary. They behaved as if it was the natural thing to do for them. They were well-versed in situations which permit one to put aside some teachings of Islam in pursuit of the fulfillment of some higher teachings. They did not refer to *Hazrat* Ayesha's leadership as coming under the context of emergency.

Alhamdulillah, I now have access to classical *hadith* literature about the early days of Islam which shows that *Hazrat* Ayesha was the leader of men in many capacities immediately after the Prophet passed away. Her leadership role culminated in the leadership of the righteous army which fought the battle of the camel (named after the camel that she was riding).

Historians agree that in the battle of the Camel (*Jaml*) Abu Bakr participated under the command of the sublime.[24]

God sent revelation to a woman

The misconception that God has throughout history sent his revelation via through men only is quite common. In a subtle way over the centuries as men came to monopolise the field of Qur'anic commentary, the belief was spread that lack of revelation to women is a sign of the superiority of men. God has however, given no sanction to this kind of male oriented thought. Nowhere in revelation are we given masculinity as a cause of God's communication, God chooses and enables on the basis of *taqwa* (consciousness and awareness of God) not on the basis of gender.

Is God male or female?

In the name of God the most gracious, the most merciful

Sura1(al-fatiha):1

Say:- God is God, the One and only. God the eternal, the Absolute. God begot not nor is begotten and there is none like unto God.

Sura 112 (llchles): 1-4

Reverence to God whom you demand your mutual (rights), and (reverence) the wombs (that carried you to birth) for God ever watches over you.

The 112 Sura expresses the unique Oneness of God. This concept contrasts sharply with the superstitious religions which have tried to "create" God in the human image. Human beings find it hard to relate to a creator who is beyond that power of human language and image making. Hence, the pagans found it necessary to make images of God. A further development of this need was the belief in incarnation. The Greeks, the Hindus, the Christians, each have a concept of God incarnating in human shape.

The Qur'an cuts the roots of anthropomorphic concepts of God by stating in one of its most powerful verses that there is none like unto God. God does not beget and hence is not female, and is not begotten like the Jesus man-child in Christian Mythology.

The use of the pronoun, "He" for God, has confused many scholars and they have gone to the extent of considering God is a male deity. From there they go on to postulate an entirely male version of Islam. However, the male verses of *sura* quoted above show that such thinking would have to be condemned as a form of shirk (associating others with God), which is the ultimate sin in Islam.

In fact, the Qur'anic terminology of God conveys not only the best male attributes but also the most female. Every chapter of the Qur'an begins with the words "In the name of God the most Gracious, the most merciful (*raheem*)". The term *raheem* is from *rahm* or the womb and conveys the totality unselfish love of a mother. This female quality is to be reverenced by Muslims. Sura Nisa, places the reverence to God and to "the wombs" (*arham*) together. With this understanding one can see how far astray from Islam are those who ridicule motherhood and try to put down women on the basis of their menstruation and bearing of children. Thus, woman is superior because only women can become mother.[25]

5

Conclusion

New Rules and Ideas about Human Rights gone

Education for every one... New thinking and interpretation for and by women

"If men cannot conceive children, then they can conceive great ideas and great works".

Why it may be asked, men use such expressions which in practically every other instance they use purely masculine phraseology and take great pain to avoid anything suggestive of the feminine? To be pregnant with ideas to be derived of a great ideas to give birth to a plan may not these other obstetrical expressions possibly indicates, when used by males, an unconscious desire to imitate the biological creativity of the female? The conversion process takes form.

Great ideas and great works be delivered of them in the form of all the things that make up our complex civilisation: art, science, philosophy, music, machinery, bridges, dams, automobiles, kitchen, gadgets and the million and one things men create and women buy. We often hear men exclaim, "That's my baby", when referring to some product of their creation, whether it be an idea or an object. It is a way of speaking and may represent merely an analogical expression, "These are the children of my brain", is another such expression. "I want to nurse this idea", is yet another. "Well, if I can't create and give birth to a biological baby, I can at least give birth to their social equivalents," is their mental consolation.

Men's drive to achievements can at least in part be interpreted as an unconsciously motivated attempt to compensate for the lack of biological creativity.

Why not Islamic feminism?

One should not be scared of the word "feminism" as our Ulama tend to be. Feminism is all about women's rights. The Qur'an is so much concerned about women's rights and superiority that it will not be wrong to say what it is the Qur'an that preached feminism for the first time and the Prophet was the first feminist ever. Obviously, "feminism" Shariah term is not old. But new terms are always welcome. The term human rights, does not exist in Shariah but today the term, "Islamic human rights" is being freely used. Why not Islamic feminism?

Woman has more wisdom than man. The Qur'an also does nowhere restrict knowledge to men alone. In fact, Ibn (knowledge) is most central to Qur'anic teachings. God is also repeatedly described in Qur'an as all-knowing and urges upon all Muslim men and women to acquire knowledge. It is as male dominated Muslim society, which restricted knowledge to men and deprived women of their fundamental right to acquire knowledge.

After India became Independent, in the early sixties onwards, communal violence broke out and that built up a sense of insecurity in the Muslims and they became insecure. Every time there was a communal riot the Muslims brooded and turned towards its own community.

Any attempt to bring about changes and reforms in the Shariah law seemed unfavourable in the community's interest.

Fearing alienation, Muslims who desired change did not refrained from raising their voices.

When A.A.A. Fyzee, a distinguished Muslim jurist, who was India's envoy to Egypt, pleaded for codification of Muslim law, he was isolated within the community. Although, he was not pleading for UCC, but only for codification, yet the community leaders were unwilling for that. Fyzee argued that the Muslim personal law widely practiced in India, was not Shariah law, enacted by any Islamic government. It was, in fact, Anglo Mohammedan law enacted by the British Government during its rule in India.

As Fyzee had made a compelling point, consequently it should not be treated as the Islamic law. In fact, post-Independence, the expressions changed and Anglo Mohammedan law came to be recognised as Muslim personal law. Therefore, it is treated as Shariah law and any attempt to alter it is met with solid resistance from the Muslim clergy.[1]

Maulvi Mumtaz Ali Advocate of Women's Rights

Maulvi sahib's arguments were quite ingenious based on his interpretation of Qur'anic verses. He so called men's superiority as *mardan ki jhuti fazilal* (false superiority of men). For example, men say (argue) that if women are equal to men why God did not grace any women with prophet-hood (*nabuwwat*)?

Mumtaz Ali Khan gives quite an ingenious reply to this argument. According to him, there have been 1,24,000 prophets and we know names of only about a dozen prophets. Similarly, his reply to the argument that why women are half the witness if they are equal to men is as follows: The Quran itself has applied this doctrine, say in case of polygamy, very rigorously and declares if you fear you cannot do justice then marry one.

Unfortunately our jurists almost, if not completely ignored it and number four (wives) become more fundamentalist than justice. And they also ignored that this verse (4:3) was revealed to do justice to widows and orphans and to ensure protection of their properties.[2]

What is worse it is men, who always do theologising, though in Islam there is no such restriction at all. Men and women are equally entitled to theologise or be *faqih* i.e. understand issues and formulate Shariah laws. But in patriarchal society men never allowed women to theologise or be *faqih*, ironically though, most of the *ahadith* have been narrated by *Hazrat* "Ayesha", the wife of the Prophet (PBOH). In history of Islam there have been several women who have been learned scholars of Islam, but not even one who founded any Shariah school.

Recently, a Conference of Muslim Personal Law Board in India, saw a huge crowd of two hundred thousand Muslims from all over Maharashtra (a state in western India) and the Chairman of the Board, Maulana Rabe Hasan Nadwi made a highly emotional speech and said that Shariah is divine and no change in it can be made even if whole Islamic world tries to change Shariah. Indian Muslims will not allow any change in it and will keep the traditional Shariah close to their chest.[3]

Recently in a poetic recital on T.V. in Saudi Arabia a Muslim poetess Hissas Hilal, burst out against the strict control regime for women in her country. It was a voice of protest and a very bold protest at that, perhaps unthinkable in her regimented society. It was, of course, in verses of the poem. She said through veiled face about Islamic preachers who sit in the position of power, but are frightening people with their *fatwas* and preying like a wolf on those seeking peace.

What is equally important is that she got loud cheers from the audience and won her a place in the competition finals. It also brought her death threats, posted on several militant websites. The *Shafi Ulaman* in religious manner are adamant on retaining strict control over women in the name of Islamia traditions women are denied their rights and free choice according to their conscience.

Another woman scholar from Iran, Laleh Baktiar, who has translated the Quran from a feminist point of view and has spent 40 years on this work, also disagrees with the translation of *daraba* as chastisement. She says after 40 years of studying and translating books related to the Quran, I realised that something was missing; an objective universal and inclusive translation of the Quran from its classical Arabic into contemporary English, most of the 17 English translations. It had been included some interpretation of the verse making a direct comparison between the English and Arabic extremely difficult. Plus many of the English translations continue to user Arabic words and names such as Allah for God, which can be confusing or even off-putting to new readers.

Two things she says about the method she followed is quite striking. She has looked at all different uses of the word in the text in context before determining the appropriate meaning in English. She used database to create 40,000 nouns and verbs of the Qur'an, and 50,000 particles of speech. This method is most appropriate as then alone one can understand the significance of a word, both as verb or noun. The methodology of understanding the Qur'an which have discovered is also collating all the verses of the Qur'an on one subject and then inferring most appropriate meaning.[4]

Personal Law in India

Muslim Personal Law Board is great news. In 2005, it was split into four and was Muslim women themselves formed two personal law boards of their own. This is big news for media and many Muslims were worried about unity of Muslim Ummah in India. The Personal Law Board itself was maintaining that it was not split, but that new boards have come into existence and no member of the existing Board had resigned and formed new board. Some members of the existing Board have even alleged that some vested interests (mainly political) are behind formation of these boards. Such stand is at least unfair accusation or at worse insulting to those who have formed these boards. It is not only Shiahs who have formed a separate board but also the Barelvis who are Sunni by sect. also this is not the best way of sorting out grievances. Instead of hurling accusations the wise leaders should try to sort out differences or solve grievances.

If today Muslim women have formed their own board it is because of gross failures of the MPCB to meet their demands which are quite just and within the Islamic framework. The triple divorce has been causing serious trouble to Muslim women. It has nothing Islamic about it. The Ulama themselves maintain that it is sinful form of divorce (*talaq-al-bida'h*) are one fails to understand why sinful practice should be perpetrated in the same Shariah.[5]

Women Delivering Sermons

Amina Wadud an Islamic scholar of repute from US led the mixed congregational prayer on 18th March 2005 in New York and also delivered *Khutiba* (i.e. sermon). It was a historic step as it was a unique development in history of Islam. Not that it was first time but it happened after centuries. Amina Wadud invoked principle of spiritual equality of men and women in Islam. She led some 130 women and men in prayer. Subsequently, another woman led Jumah prayer and delivered a sermon in Canada too. Asra Nomani, a former Wall Street, journalist also led prayer in a University in the Boston area in the USA. In fact, Asia was main motivator behind the movement for a woman leading the mixed gender project.

Prophet's *hadith* also allows a woman to lead congregational prayer. The Holy Prophet has asked Umme Waraqah bint Abdullah to lead prayer in her house, which included men. She was well versed in Quran compared to others including men and hence the Prophet (PBUH) asked her to lead the congregational prayer. Now generally *dar* (house) is interpreted as her family and according to this interpretation she was asked to lead her family members in prayer including her husband. But it is also stated in *Hadith* that the Prophet (PBUH) applauded a *mu'addin* (caller to the prayer) who was a man. This means it was not only her family but most probably her locality. Her day should not mean household or family by locality as dar-ul-Islam would not mean family of Islam locality even a country of Islam.

But a woman can be greater (*'alimah*) than a man and it was on this principal that the prophet (PBUH) allowed her to lead mixed congregational prayer. It was 1400 years ago in twenty-first century there is such opposition to a woman leading the prayer. It is really strange. Stranger reasons are being given to oppose a woman leading mixed congregational prayer.

A leading Arab alim Sheikh Yusuf al Qardawi says in his fatwa that 'throughout' Muslim history it has never been heard of a woman leading the Friday prayer of delivering the Friday sermon, even during the era when a woman shagavat Ad-Durr, was ruling the Muslim in Egypt during the Mamluk period. It is established that leadership in prayer in Islam is to be for men. His argument is well established that leadership in prayer in Islam is to be for men.

Qardawi further argues "Hence, it is to avoid the stirring instincts of men that the Shariah dictates that only men can call for prayer and lead people in the prayer and that women's rows in prayer be behind the men". This may be Sheikh's view it is certainly not the Quran's and Sunnah's view Qardawi thinks the Prophet did not know what he knows about the men's sexuality and permitted Umm Waraqan to lead prayer. And he also thinks that only men's sexual urge can be stirred not women when they pray behind men.[6]

Meanwhile, Muslim women are on the move in various Muslim countries. In every Muslim country and countries with considerable Muslim population like India education is fast among Muslim women. This certainly brings increased awareness among women themselves and they press for their rights both Islamic as well as secular. There are both types of movements in the Islamic world. In some Muslim countries Muslim women theologians have emerged with thorough knowledge of the Quran, Islamic theology and Shariah. There are women theologians like Fatima and Riffat Hassam from the USA and several others. Also there are women's organisations like "sisters in Islam" from Malaysia.

These women theologians and organisations are questioning the traditional interpretation of Quran in respect of women's right and developing new feminine oriented theology ensuring equal rights for men and women. "Sisters-in-Islam" from Malaysia is challenging orthodox Ulama from Malaysia. They are even trying to get the concept of marital rape accepted as a valid law. Bangladesh though otherwise quite poor and backward is not far behind. There recently twenty female officers have completed two years grueling military training and passes out from Bangladesh Military Academy (BMA).[7]

Mosque as a place of refuge and rest for women

Ayesha reports that then the girl came to the messenger of God (peace and blessing of God be upon him) and embraced Islam. Ayesha adds: "She (the new *muslimah*) a little corner and a little tent for herself in the mosque (*fis masjid*). She used to come to me and converse with me. When she sat by me, she would say: the day of the satchel was from the strange power of our creator: Listen! It saved me from the city of *kufr*. Ayesha says when I asked her why she always said so, she told me her story.

Mosques belong to God, not to any individual or government.

Now if someone says that Muslim women should not visit mosques or should not be part of the decision-making processes for the administration of mosques, such a person is violating the commands of God and is saying something for which God has given no permission.

Male right has been clearly rejected by the Prophet Mohammad (peace and blessings of God be on him), "Even is the male involved is the husband of the women, he has no right to stop her from going to the mosque".

If women stop going to the mosque, half the Muslim community gets cut off from Islamic efforts. There might be difficulties in visiting the mosque. Madina was not lighted by electricity. Even then women are not to be stopped from going.[8]

For instance, a *hadith* collected by *baihaqi*, in which a woman was commanded by the Holy Prophet to pray inside her own home and not in the Masjid-e-Nabawi, is the centre piece of the *hadith* teaching of our scholars,. They disregard the fact that this *hadith* was not accepted by Bukhari or Muslims or Malik and is in any case related to an exceptional case. By contrast our scholars disregard, or de-emphasise all those *hadith* which forbid men from stopping the women from going to the mosque.

Islamic dress and modesty are ordained for both men and women. Proper dress is part of the overall Islamic scheme to let Muslims, men and women, relate to each other as brothers and sisters in the Islamic movement (or as fathers and mothers depending on their age factor). Modesty was not meant to create two different worlds, one for men and another for women. It is owing to this artificially created separation that men and women in the Muslim world often do not know how to deal with each other. One scholar tries to create the impression that the alternative to separation is the corrupt (bikinis, dating, illegitimate children), world of the women in the West. I have published a number of *hadith* which indicate that the Islamic movement endorses neither complete separation nor the complete mixing. There can be no genuine Islamic movement unless men and women learn to deal with each other on a human level; both free mixing and complete separation are anti-Islamic.

Trying to minimise her role as moral leader of the Muslim community, and even gone to the shameful extent of accusing her of violating the teachings of the Qur'an. Average Muslims who do not have access to the histories of early Islam do not know that Ayesha our spiritual mother, used to teach *sahaba*, even the most learned of them. When Ayesha led the army from Mecca to Basra, she was followed not only by some of the most renowned *sahaba*, like Talha and Zubair, but also by numerous second generation scholars of the Quran. None of them made the claim, which our "scholars" have made that she had no right to lead the Muslims. If modern Muslims can understand the example of "Ayesha", they will know where our scholars have gone wrong.

We need to set up organisations in which the pure unadulterated teachings of the Qur'an and the authentic *hadith* will be put into practice. Women should be equal participants in such organisations. Women who practice Islam, who combine *taqwa* (piety) with *'Ilm'* (learning) should be able to become Ameers and members of the Shoora, if the members wish to elect them to these positions. There is no Islamic obstacle in the way of women serving at the highest position. The man's thought is that a woman cannot be a judge is baseless as far as the Qur'an and the authentic *hadith* are concerned.[9]

God says in Quran, *"Let those who fight in the cause of God, who sell life of this world for the hereafter: to him who fights in the cause of God, whether he is slain or gets victory, soon shall we give a great reward. And why should you not fight in the cause of God and those who being weak, are ill-treated (and oppressed)? Men, women and children, whose cry is: "Our Lord! Rescue us from this town, whose people are oppressors, and raise for us from The one who will help!"*

*"Those who believe fight in the cause of God and those who reject faith, fight in the cause of evil: so fight against the friends of Satan: feeble indeed is the cunning of Satan". (*4:74-76*)*

God says in the Quran:

"The Believers, men and women, are protectors and helpers, one another, they enjoin what is just and forbid what is evil, they perform regular prayers, practice regular charity, and obey God and His messenger. On them will God pour mercy, for God is exalted in power!"

The Historical Reasons for the Oppression of Women

During the early years of Islam in Mecca, in spite of the tribal and oppressive situation of the first 55 who accepted Islam nine were women. The first martyr in Islam was a woman Summaya. After the Prophet passed away, Ayesha his wife known as the mother of all believers became the greatest teacher of Islam to the Muslims. Even the greatest companions of the Prophet used to come to her for the Islamic guidance.

As participants in the struggle, we must always be careful in following Islamic guidance about modesty and free mixing. God says in Qur'an 24:30-31 that the believing men and the believing women should guard their modesty.

During the last 15 years, I have researched the classical *tafsir* and *hadith* literature in depth, almost on a daily basis. My findings are as follows:

1. The traditional *Ulema* have concentrated on those verses of Qur'an which were revealed at the early stage of the process which finally emancipated Muslim women. For instance, the famous Qur'anic verse of our *Ulema* 4:34. As opposed to this they totally ignore 9:71, which is the

final revelation in which the mutual role of men and women is mentioned. The classical Tafsirs, like Ibn Kathir's, simply ignore the facts that the words believing women are mentioned in this verse. Even those *mufassiren* (commentators) who usually so their *tafsir* by discussing the nuances of each word somehow ignore the mention of believing women as the *awillyya* of men in 9:71. The modern commentators who are traditional, though very selective in their approach like of 9:7. Even the Mandoodi failed to notice that like oath does not include obedience to the husband in the oath.

2. Some verses of Qur'an are quoted out of context by our *Ulema* and then are popularised to such an extent that the impression is created that they are absolute commands of God. For instance, after divorce men can remarry immediately while women have to wait for three measured menstrual cycles to avoid problems relating to paternity. This teaching is contained in 2:228. It has nothing to do with mutual roles of men and women as equals or inferior. But our "scholars" pick up a few words from this verse *wa-lir-Rijale `alaihinna darajat,* and try to conceal the fact that he verse is about post-divorce issues. The verses following 2:228 are also about divorce. Thus, our "scholar" are guilty of *tahrif* or unabashed distortion of the Qur'an.

3. The traditional scholars have committed serious errors of omission and commission in the way they have presented *hadith* to the Muslims. In fact, the traditional dealings with *hadith* gives such an ugly picture of Islam that as a reaction an entire movement that of "modernists" led by Dr Fazlur Rehman (now in Chicago), has risen to question *hadith* as a source of Islamic law. My findings is that *hadith* is essential to Islam. It must be placed second to the Quran, but if it is discarded as a source of Islamic law, irreparable damage will be done to the essential teachings of Islam.

Hadith literature supports the equality of Muslim men as women. Here too the traditionalists (not to be confused with traditionalists) have totally de-emphasised *hadith* which gives equality to men and women. At the same time these scholars, to be found in every existing school of thought, have treated some isolated *hadith*, as the case of Islamic teachings. For instance, a *hadith* collected by Bailquis, in which a woman was commanded by the holy Prophet to pray inside her own home and not in Masjid-e-Nabawi, is the centre piece of the *hadith* teaching of our scholars. I disregard the fact that this *hadith* was not accepted by Bukhari or Muslam or Malik and is any case related to an exceptional case. By contrast our scholars disregard, or de-emphasise all those *hadith* which forbid men from stopping the women from going to the mosque.

4. Islamic dress and modesty are ordained for both men and women. Proper dress is over all Islamic scheme to let Muslim men and women to relate to each other as brothers and sisters in the Islamic movement (or fathers or mothers depending on the age).

   Modesty was not meant to create two different worlds, one for men and one for women. It is owing to this artificial separation created that men and women often do not know how to deal with each other. Our scholars try to create the impression that the alternative to separation is corrupt (biknis, dating, illegitimate children), world of the women in the west. There can be no genuine Islamic movement unless men and women learn to deal with each other on a human level, birth free mixing and complete separation are anti-Islamic.

   Modesty is not meant just for women, nor does Islam endorse double standards for men and women. The punishment for adultery and fornication are exactly the same for men and women. The extra covering for head was meant to dignify women and to stop men from approaching them as sex objects.

Islam certainly does not endorse the attitude of Muslim men who pretend that every women with her head uncovered must be of a "loose character".

In fact, a *hadith* from Bukhari, which indicates the holy Prophet, emphatically commanded women to go forth to participate in many prayers and good works. Such authentic *hadith* take care of the so called scholars of Islam that Islam does not allow women to go outside their homes to participate in any activity in which men are present or to uncover their faces.

5. Ayehsa Siddiqqua in her life and teachings has provided humanity with the best example of a Muslim woman. She did not bear children, but she is described as the mother of the believers, because in Islam the best mother is the one who can teach and Ayesha was the best teacher and example for Muslim women. She is the biggest "problem" for both the traditional sunni and shia scholars. Both of them have tried to 're-write' history by trying to minimise her role as moral leader of the Muslim community, and even gone to the shameful extent of accusing her of violating the teachings of the Quran. Average Muslim who do not have access to the history of early Islam do not know that Ayesha, our spiritual mother, used to teach sahib even the most learned of them. When 'Ayesha' led the army from Mecca to Basra, she was followed not only by the most renowned *sahaba*, but also by numerous, second generation scholars of the Quran.[10]

Islamic Feminism – Women's Superiority in Quran

When women were educated and their awareness of equality with men found no response in the society and they found themselves subservient to men an aggressive feminist movement arose. Feminists have developed more balanced view point. Women's position today has improved thanks to the pressure of the feminist movement. Still, in the most western countries women are not elected to high political offices.

In Muslim countries the situation of women is despicable. In Saudi Arabia they are not allowed to vote. They are not even allowed to drive. Women in Kuwait won the right to vote recently, after prolonged struggle. In several Muslim countries such as Egypt, Jordan, Pakistan etc., women continue to be killed in the name of family honour if they try to marry a man of their choice or even found talking to some male friend.

There is thus an urgent need for Islamic feminist movement. Islam has given those rights to be, right to marry, right to divorce, right to own property, right to earn their living, right to education and right to inherit. Unfortunately, all these rights are being denied to them by the so called keepers of faith. In Islam these rights existed all along but the male dominated society never allowed women to avail them. Not long ago, the leading Islamic seminary to Deoband issued a fatwa that Muslim women cannot contest elections but modified it later by saying they have to observe veil while campaigning. It is also to be noted that there is no concept of veil in Qur'an; there is only the concept of dignified dressing. However, Muslims everywhere force veil on their women. The Qur'anic verse (24:31) makes it very clear that what should be displayed and what should not be displayed.

The Islamic feminist discourse has to articulate all these rights given to women by the Quran and if there happens to be any grey area, it has to be subjected to fresh interpretation in the light of contemporary development. Such a discourse does not alleviate from the Qur'anic rights and at the same time does not accept male point of view through interpreting the Qur'an. Women must not only acquire Qur'anic feminist narrative. However, it is high time that Muslim women acquire deep, Islamic Eldership, mastery over Qur'anic and Arabic knowledge and launch Islamic feminist movement. Marriage in Islam is not a subordinate relationship between a man and a woman but an equal partnership, both being part of mutual obligations. She cannot be divorced arbitrarily, as is the practice today. Marriage has been described by the Qur'an as "strong bond" (4:21), which one cannot break at husband's whim.

Moreover, Islamic feminist discourse should empower women to make choice whether they want a child or not on grounds of health, family, size and economic capability. A man cannot force woman to go on bearing children, as she is much more than a child bearing machine. As Islamic feminist discover has to be pro-choice for women. Thus, Islamic feminist discourse is not only justified but is also quite essential to empower her to achieve for human dignity as accorded to her by the Quran.[11]

Oppositions to Reform in Muslim personal law comes mainly because of reasons like:–

1. Recurring, communal violence that makes Muslims feel insecure and any change in their law is seen as a threat to their religious identity. It is true that reform and change can be more effective and acceptable if people feel secure.

2. Muslims are by and large quite poor and illiterate. Their economic plight is worse than that of dalits, though modern professionals are also emerging from this backward economic base.

3. Women of Muslim community are not educated in most cases and more often than not, confined to household work and thus lack consciousness of their rights even Islamic. Rights.

4. So far, secular elements and secular feminism had demanded implementation of UCC, but from late eighties

onwards some of them were co-opted by the Hindutva forces. The BJP, the Hindu communal party, made promulgation of UCC a part of the Hindutva agenda.

5. It is not only Muslims alone who follow personal law but all communities including the Hindus who are the majority community follow their respective personal laws.

In fact, there is no dual system in India as far as personal laws are concerned. No community follows UCC in India. Hence there is no civil law for others and personal law or Shariah law is applicable to Muslims only. The only difference is that Hindus, the majority community has reformed their traditional law. Marriage is considered a sacrament among Hindus giving away one's daughter is called *kanyadaan* (i.e. donating the girl to her husband) and since it is sacramental no divorce is possible. The reforms enacted in the traditional Hindu law gave women rights of marriage, divorce, inheritance and property and also banned polygamy and allowed widow remarriage.

But in Islam, many of these rights were already available to Muslims. A Muslim woman has rights of marriage, divorce (with certain conditions in Shariah law), property and inheritance (she inherits as daughter, wife and as mother). Thus, Islamic law is most progressive as compared to other religions and traditional laws of India. However, it does not mean that there are no problems with Shariah law.

Most of the Muslim women suffer mainly on account of triple divorce. Polygamy is a problem but not as acute as triple divorce. The Muslim personal law board, which has been set up by some Muslims continue to be dominated by some highly conservative Muslims. Though triple divorce is called *talaq-i-bidah* (a sinful form of divorce), still it is enforced.

Many husbands pronounce *talaq* thrice in a state of anger or even drunken state. Despite this it is held valid. Every other Muslim country has abolished this law, but, India with its about 140 million of Muslim population holds it valid. Only Ahl-i-hadith and Shiah Muslims don't practice it. All efforts to persuade the Muslim Personal Law Board (MPLB) to agree to abolish it have been in vain. Let alone abolish it, they are not even prepared to educate the Muslim masses that it is sinful practice and hence should not be resorted to.

The only silver lining in the otherwise dark cloud is that Muslim women are taking to education in large numbers, which is bringing more awareness among them about their rights. Some Muslim women NGOs have been campaigning for women's rights. There are, NGOs who reject religion as an opinion and campaign for gender equality on secular lines. Yet there are some other that take religion seriously and campaign for gender equality on the basis of re-interpretation of Islamic Shariah.

But now time has come to realise this Qur'anic ideal. The Muslim world however is not mentally prepared for implementation of the Qur'anic ideal even today. But modern education is preparing Muslim women for realisation of Qur'anic ideal. Yet at best it can be a long struggle to realise the Qur'anic ideal of gender superiority. Yet a beginning has been made through awareness campaign among Muslim women.

There is also a need for Islamic feminists view point. So far only men have interpreted the Qur'an and there are no major interpretational endeavours on the part of women. Islam does not prohibit women from reading and revisiting Qur'an. In fact, Qur'anic ideal can be realised only through feminist interpretation.

At the end, I would like to say that India a liberal, secular and a democratic country can be a fertile ground for such feminist endeavour. It is not possible in any Islamic country to realise this ideal as there is no freedom of thought.

The conservative Ulama dominate the entire space. It is countries like India, which provide free and creative space for women to enjoy. The absence of UCC can be more than compensated by re-interpreting the Shariah laws and practicing gender equality. Future surely holds quite a bit of promise in this.

All this has increased awareness among Muslim women regarding their plight, who have now started exerting pressure for a change in laws pertaining to marriage, divorce, inheritance, rape and so on. This is another important factor that plays a crucial role in the formation of NGOs for women. These NGOs are elucidating women regarding their rights organising them and fighting cases on their behalf. Muslim women are no exception to this role. All India Muslim dominated body of conservative *Ulama*. All the options of the Board are based on the medieval texts evolved mainly by male interpretation of the Qur'an and *Hadith*. Women had little role to play in the formulation of their Shariah laws. Today the medieval text cannot be enforced mechanically. It has to be thoroughly rethought in modern context.[12]

In Islam women have every right not only to recite the Qur'an but also to interpret it 'jihad' (creative interpretation) in every Muslim's religious rights given proper knowledge and understanding of the text and causes of its revelation. As scholars of Islam know every verse in the Qur'an was revealed in response to some questions in the minds of believers then Muslims should not understand the Qur'anic verses in response to their own situation.

The Feminist Viewpoint

In her book *'The Forgotten Queens of Islam'*, Moroccan feminist and sociologist Fatima Mernissi argues that gradually, over time women were declared, strangers to the place of worship. She calls this a betrayal to the Prophet whose mosque in Madinah was open to all welcoming all those interested in Islam, including women, Mernissi traces the writings of various authoritative imams down through the centuries to demonstrate how this happened.

Mernissi concluded her foray into history with an impassioned plea to uncover the marginalised voices of not only women, but also peasants and the poor. It is, she suggests the currents of resistance and counter resistance from these quarters which are never reflected in Islam's official discourse.

In Fatima Mernissi, then, we find a women's re-reading or history: a tracing of the path of women's marginalisation through a critical selection and re-assessment of *hadith*. In her analysis, the ground has shifted from what Islam does or does not say, to who has said what on behalf of Islam and for what purpose. The importance of recovering women's history is part of feminist agenda; a necessary move to counteract attempts to legitimise women's subordination. We hear a similar echo in the words of a December 1995, resolution from the All India Democratic Women's Association, "The Holy Qur'an" is considered as the divine revelation by Muslim is therefore sacrosanct. But the interpretation of the Qur'an and the *hadith* is not.

In the same *hadith,* for example, it refers to woman leaving before men from the mosque clothed in outer garments which kept them from being recognised, or women praying behind the men of her household, or women keeping their heads lowered in prayer until men raised theirs in order to preserve modesty, or occasions on which the Prophet advised women to refrain from using scent or to keep their dress and ornaments simple when coming to the mosque. In all these different *hadith* it is clear that women were praying in the mosques during the times of the Prophet.

Although, some women argue unreservedly for women's place in mosque, others adopt a more provisional view. In fact, some of those who acknowledge women right, encourage, women not to make use of it. In a letter to the editor of the popular Radiance View Weekly, Waheed H. Hashmi of

Hyderabad writes that women have a right to offer their prayers at a mosque, including during the congregational prayer time as long as they occupy a place from where they cannot be seen by men. The writer adds, however that women should not go because "mixed congregations of both the sexes tend to breed evil thoughts in human minds".

This is also the opinion of Abdussattar Yusuf Shaikh, the Secretary of the conservative All India Muslim Personal Law. Abdussattar Yusuf Shaikh, admits that the practice of women praying at the mosque is not "un-Islamic" but it is better if women stay in *purdah* and pray at home[13].

Three Major Strategies to Address Concerns of Women

- At one end of the spectrum are two neo-traditionalists strategies, one conservative and the other reactionary. They are "traditional" in so far as they both uphold the pristine honour attributed to women as articulated within classical texts such as at Ghazali's book on marriage and sexuality (1984). Traditionally a woman was dependent upon a male member of society, usually her father or husband, for establishing her legitimacy and maintaining her social honour. She was not considered as autonomous agent. In both of the neo-traditionalist strategies, the Muslim woman is perceived only in terms relative to the man's home, a pious or recalcitrant wife, mother, daughter or home-maker, in the context of the mass urbanisation affecting many Muslim countries.

- Paid employment for women is no longer simply necessary for lower classes. More Muslim women leave their homes for paid employment than did directly after the end of colonialism. Decent and comfortable lifestyle increasingly depends on a woman's contribution to the family income. In addition as women increase their levels of education and their professional capabilities, they become better informed and more active participants in the public sectors of society. Some Muslim governments support women's valuable contributions in the greater interest of national productivity and development. This in no way indicates that national interests are Islamic.

- Both the neo-traditionalists approaches address the issue of Muslim women's identity experiences and concerns over equitable rights and responsibilities by asserting that "Islam" provided women their full rights more than 14 centuries ago. They offer little concrete consideration or analysis of the innumerable instances when those rights are denied to women in the real context of lived Islam. Such a consideration would require a critical examination of the way the word Islam is used. When "Islam" is applied to the status quo, it makes it difficult for women to address this ambiguity of usage without being seen as recalcitrant.[14]

One significant blind spot was the complete voiceless position of women in the historical legacy of "*tafsir*". Furthermore, the gap that came from the voiceless position of women in *tafsir*, a major Islamic intellectual discipline, cannot be closed with a mere rhetoric of equality in Islam. Closing this gap will be a major contribution to the current debates over the status of women in Islam. A vision of authentic Islamic development is predicted, upon the historical struggles of Muslim who participated fully in that development. The absence of the female voice with regard to the Qur'an has severely affected the very notions many Muslim hold of the Creator and consequently, of the notion they have about the purpose and role of human kind in creation.

Although many Muslim males may not perceive their privileged status as a disadvantage, those Muslims most comfortable with previous interpretive methods and conclusions are adversely affected by the gender disparity that was the consequences of the exclusive participation of men in *tafsir*.

Although the Qur'an does not advocate slavery, all of its discussions about it take the institutions for granted and focus on fair and just treatment of slaves. The text also includes incentives for free men and women to grant freedom to slaves as part of the duty and spirit of Islam or for the expiation, of certain religious infractions.

Although Muslims extended into these global discussions, no claim was made as a Qur'anic precedent existed for the rights of all human beings to live free from slavery. Neither did Muslims resist this global trend toward recognising freedom as an aspect of human dignity by maintaining that the absence of a Qur'anic statement that meant the institution should not be abolished. When slavery became virtually obsolete, globally it did so with no particular assistance or resistance of Muslims. This is a strange parody. Despite the absence of any Qur'anic argument in favour of abolishing slavery, the Muslims world responded positively to its abolition and recognised it as a significant movement toward human dignity.

Meanwhile, Muslims remain paralysed against the grossly inferior status experienced by women in the context of many Muslim nations-states, despite extensive textual precedent for establishing the full human dignity of women.[15]

Female experiences and Perspective

Two questions beg to be asked – What difference does it make? And ... Can we correct this error at the present time?

One can never sufficiently recreate the historical female voice with regards to women's experience of the Qur'an; the record simply too sparse. The text still exists in its original form; however, critical thinking still manages to be a component of human intellect. It could be possible to begin critical consideration of the significance of female voice in the text and the female perspective on what it means to follow the guidance of the text that in what it means to be Muslim. Both these important tasks considering the female voice within the Qur'an and female responses to the text are in their initial stages.

The perspective of an individual with regard to a circumstance is affected by his or her relationship to that circumstance as in the familiar analogy of four blind persons feeling different parts of an animal and coming to different conclusions about the nature of the animal. Still the whole of the animal is more than its constituent parts. Adding all four perceptions together still leaves a blind spot because the animals totality is greater when integrated with the elephants animate and dynamic nature. A similar metaphysical component is essential to the Muslim ethos. The Qur'an states, *"Perhaps you hate a thing in which God has placed much good" (2:216).* This implies that one's personal perspectives on an issue should not be the sole means for evaluating its worth. Yet, one's perceptions are powerful enough that one sometimes elevates them to objects of worship, *"Have you not seen those (objects of worship)?" (Qur'an 25:43).* Although, strongly influenced by their perceptions, humans must temper those perceptions with the wisdom of guidance and the discipline of physical and metaphysical experience.

When the Qur'an states: *"God does not change a condition of a people until they first change what is within their own souls" (13:11),* it indicates the human potential for higher and more dynamic levels of perception and consciousness. In turn these changes must lead to and be led by social, cultural and moral development. Growth and development in technology demonstrates that human awareness has been transformed into new vistas, so likewise human system of social justice must be transformed.[16]

Amina was so right when she states that God does not change the condition of the people until they don't change what is within their own souls. It's high time women demand gender jihad, total new interpretation like her the total change in woman position in every aspect of life.

Women voices are so silent because if they speak they are bad women. So now all together shoulder to shoulder with our daughters, sisters, mothers, daughter-in-law, demand gender jihad. Their demand should be they should get what Qur'an wants them to get.

Muslims remain paralysed against the inferior presentation through them in Qur'an. They are comfortable with previous interpretation but like slavery is gone women have to come up together and prove that women are better than men. No inferiority complex for any woman around us, we should stand proud and superior.

General Rights

To many Muslims the Qur'an is the Magna Carta of human rights and a large part of it concern is to free human beings from the (religious, political, economic or nay other). Tribalism, racism, sexism, slavery or anything else that prohibits or inhibits human beings from actualising the Qur'anic vision of human destiny embodied in the classic proclamation, *"Towards God is thy limit" (Qur'an 53:42).* And is my limit too.

In the section entitled "General Rights", which follows an account, is given of the Qur'an's affirmation of fundamental rights that all human beings ought to possess, because they are so deeply rooted in our humanness that their denial or violation is tantamount to a negation or disregard of that which makes people human. From the perspective of the Qur'an, these rights came into existence when people were created, people who were by God, so that human potential could be actualised. Rights created or given by God cannot be abolished by any temporal rules or human agency. Eternal and immutable, they ought to be exercised because everything that God does is for a just purpose.

While constantly enjoying all the Qur'an goes beyond this concept *ihsan*, which literally means "restoring the balance by making up a loss or deficiency (Parwez 1977, 78).

To understand this concept it is necessary to understand the nature of the ideal society or community (*ummah*), envisaged by the Qur'an. The word *ummah* comes from the root word umm or 'mother'. The symbols of a mother and motherly love and compassion are also linked with the two attributes most characteristic of God, namely, *rahim* and *rahman*, both of which are derived from the root *'rahm'* meaning 'womb'. The ideal *ummah* cares about all its members just as an ideal mother cares about all her children. Knowing that all are not equal that each has different needs, although showing undue favour to any child would be unjust, a mother who gives to a handicapped child more than she does to her other child or children, is not acting unjustly but is exemplifying the spirit of *ihsan* by helping to make up the deficiency of a child who needs special assistance in meeting the requirements of life. *Ihsan*, thus, shows God's sympathy for the disadvantaged segments of human society (such as women, orphans, slaves, the poor, the infirm and the minorities).[17]

The world needs peace and prosperity, wisdom and education to understand each other only women can provide this heavenly earth of no fight among nations, no child hungry, no girl child/woman slavery, no money spent on war, women design to talk and solve problem through thinking, understanding and love. Our brain is happy brain, not like men who hate everybody and angry all the time with their false superiority complex. They are ready to fight and torture child and woman. It does not prove you are superior. It proves you are not a human being, but a very bad animal and you tell yourself you are a superior being in God's image. God should be ashamed that God made man because you are not human any more. You are an animal when you torture women. You forget that your first word was "Mom". When you started walking if we women had not held your hand you would have fallen down. We feed you from a little baby to a mature man, and you develop a bad hand. When a woman sees a child is crying they run to the child to calm them down, this is a proof of the superiority that a woman shows.

- When you see a child crying you torture or kill them, again proving that you are not God but worse than an animal. I teach my son to be well mannered with all the women and daughters like a mother and a superior being. If we all "ma" think alike me and treat their daughters and daughters-in-law we are proud of you prove your superiority.
- Everyone has a job trying to help save girls from boys but we have to stand together and teach our daughters self defence.
- Now we have new technology, monitoring every house so that they can be safe. We never allow children to be slave we must free them before men torture them and make them slave.
- Then we prove our superiority we are not going to listen to the men anymore we are going to save the world and girl child.
- We never allow our husband to go the bad way nor our son. I believe women fail to save women. They are from Prime Minister to police if we promise each other and ourselves you never allow men to reach to do slavery or bad things. No war, no more slavery. To free women before any harm come to them is our duty. We hit them back if they are harassing us. We women have to end these men's bad behaviour from childhood never let them treat women badly. There is no other time left for the world is deteriorating to become worst everywhere we see men of bad behaviour mother can punish their sons if they are not behaving properly if they are not well with women. I know that everybody is not treated like me, but in home itself women are treated badly by first

their fathers then their brothers and then their husbands and finally their sons, but if we change and treat our daughters the very best and mother like a mother, then I hope you can teach men. Your house should be changes if they are not like my house. Women should be treated well - daughter or daughter-in-law or mother alike. You can tell father and son to behave well and brother also, for we do not want them to become monsters.

- If we believe in superiority, we can handle it. But daughter/daughter-in-law/mother and grandmother should stand up to the monster man. All are responsible. Mother is not raising them to be monsters but the three men - son, father and husband - we want them to be gentlemen.
- If our son is not the monster man then they are not afraid to accept we are superior being and our family, society, job and country.
- Women of the world have to stand with me to walk into the new hand in hand, peace, justice, prosperity under superior women.
- Everybody respects each other, when our sons are perfect and then our world is perfect.
- We are now living in the new era, new interpretation of Qur'an. Now we are moving into good cause now justice and care for everybody, like in Qur'an.

Today, women are highly aware of their rights and such practices are against principle of equality which is more fundamental than any Arab practice. Still it is practiced in countries like India and even thought to be divine. Similarly, polygamy is much misused and also thought to be man's privilege. It has to be regulated and should not be allowed to be used as per ones whims and fancies. No woman accepts it today. Patriarchal values are being challenged especially by women.[18]

Personal Law

It was a huge gathering of the Muslim Personal Law Board (MPLB), in Mumbai, 22nd April 2012. It was three days conference from 20 April to 22 April and lot of efforts was made through announcements in the mosques local professions and individual efforts to mobilise, in support of MPLB, and to prove its clout as usual emotional speeches were made to warn government against interference in Muslim Personal Law, called Shari–at-e–mutahhira (Holy Shariat). It is interesting that this time the word Holy was added to what is usually called Shariat, possibly to emphasise its divine character. Maulana Rabi Hasan Nadwi president of the MPLB, made a highly emotional speech and said Muslim will lay down their lives if government interfere in the Holy Shariat and that even if whole Islamic world makes changes in the Holy Shariat, Indian Muslims will not allow any change in it and will continue to embrace as it is without any change. Of course, this emotional rhetoric great ago a fly how it appeals to the masses, who hardly know anything about the way Shariat law came into existence, and for them the words of *Ulama* are like divine words.

Why talk about Muslim countries the Fiqh Academy New Delhi recently held an international conference in Mhow and decided in presence of *Ulama* and eminent Islamic jurists that Muslim, women are entitled to Khula, if they insist on it, without permission from then husband. Also a few day ago a fatwa from Darul Uoom Deoband advised the person who asked whether he could take another wife while first wife he is married to, is alive as far as possible. Generally polygamy is considered in India as man's privilege. These changes are taking place and must take place in the changed circumstances.

A great 'Alim (theologian and jurist) from Qatar Allama Yusuf Qardawi has published a book in which he says that fatwas can and must be changed with the change of place and circumstances and has given ten different grounds in which this fatwas can be changed. He pleads that one should deeply reflect on changes of place and circumstances, before issuing any fatwa. Allama Qardawi is highly respected alim of the Islamic world. Does Yusuf Qardawi not know that Shari'at is divine? Shari'at is as much divine as it is also human as much as it is also based on human interpretations of these divine sources. And to that extent it must change, with the change in places and circumstances as Allama Yusuf Qardawi insists.[19]

World needs peace and prosperity, wisdom and education, to understand each other and only women can provide this heaven on earth. No fight among nations, no child dying, no money for war. A woman's mind is designed to solve problems through communication and sympathy. A woman's brain is a happy brain not like men's brain, which hates everybody and is angry all the time, with the force of a superiority complex. They always think that they are right and always ready to fight. When you insult a woman it does not prove your superiority it only proves you are an inferior being but an animal.

With their false ego men lost their humanity. Men should realise when you torture a woman, the first word you spoke was 'mother', and when you walk your mother holds your little hands so you can walk properly, and then you become bad monster man with false superiority. When your mother feeds you and your body becomes strong because of your mother who is a female.

When you put down girls and women, somehow I feel this is like putting down your mother. I feel this is also your mother's fault because from the time you were a baby she should have taught you to be gentle and respect girls and make you feel proud for respecting women, like I teach my son and am more proud of my daughter for being a woman. We don't need a monster man, but we need a perfect gentleman for the world like my son and my husband. But all women should feel proud of being a woman. Since childhood men's false sense of superiority has to go. I am asking all mothers of the world to teach your sons to be good and be proud of your daughters and daughters-in-law. We should not hurt our daughters-in-law for our son's sake. We have to stop girls slavery only if we can use our brain for safety through our brain power. It is you yourself who allow your son to ill treat your daughter-in-law. All daughters-in-law must learn self-defence.

We cannot depend on men we have to do it together to ensure full education and the best job available for the girl. Through new technology we now monitor our girls for their safety. Our daughters have to be your priority and not men. Home is the place where everything starts either good or bad, for men and for women, we mothers have to decide. They are putting women down for thousands of years, but newly with us, the female persons together, fighting for rights and superiority.

We have to change the men's society to girls' society we need all the power from the word woman and together. If society changes then man realises their bad behaviour. There is no other time left to teach the boys how to behave like a human and like God wants us to behave with each other.

Mothers can punish their sons so that they can never raise hand on a woman. I never hit my son, but taught my son never disrespect women, but treat them with respect.

Mothers should insist and teach their sons to respect women even if they are their servant. Son has to feel that you are very that you are a woman and you are proud of you are daughters too. Doesn't matter how your father treated you or your brothers. You have to change now. If you didn't like your father's behaviour make sure it is not repeated with your daughters now. You should now be proud of your daughters and yourself. Now, you are in charge of your house. You don't want your son to grow up as a monster. You are a superior woman, so make him realise that you are the superior being. Mothers have to teach daughters-in-law and love them because they are your kind of species. Don't hate them for your son's sake. Don't hate your own species.

It is every woman's responsibility to make their little boys not monster men but into dream men.

Other than North India and Africa, most of the countries consider woman as equal to man. They don't need boys to do everything even if it is religious activity. Even girls can give funerals. They can perform religious duties in the graveyard; if society builds the woman for the woman then men have to give up that bad behaviour towards women.

When we have superiority about our mother we can teach them how to be with girls and boys and prepare them for the new world. My request I am asking all the sisters obey God not man. We all have to learn self-defence and education.

Marriage should be secondary thing in girl's life. We know society is not going to change in a day but only we women can change society as soon as possible. We have to believe in women power and make our daughters believe in that power. Or son should not be a monster man but he should be the perfect man with the perfect respect for the women. When we make our home perfect, our society and our country are all going to be perfect and gentle society and country.

Women of the world have to stand with me and march into a new world with peace, justice and prosperity for all. No crying, no war when everybody has education and prosperity.

Slavery is abolished by still we have little boys and girls still we have to abolish every kind of slavery. We are living in a new era with a new interpretation of Qur'an that has a new outlook towards women. We are looking into a cause like justice and care for everything. Through the Qur'an we are not only an equal gender but a superior gender and we are not afraid. We are not going to need man made interpretation of the Qur'an.

Man made society not Qur'an made working for rich men only all over the world. It only pleased their ego to put women down. The Qur'an has a tax for rich people called Zakat for the poor. Which means the tax is supposed to be spent on the poor people and the just society but they spend them on war.

Qur'an prescribed their tax for rich people so that need of the poor will be met and they don't go hungry. America has this tax. But the Qur'an already has this tax in the Sixth century A.D. in which the rich people paid the tax for the poor people.

The taxes are supposed to be spent on school and food for the poor, but man-made society is using these funds for themselves only.

Qur'an says other things regarding:

Will: that when a person dies his property and money is to be divided among all in the family.

(Husband/wife/son/daughter/uncle/aunt)

But for that when a man dies all the property goes to the elder son. Qur'an does not want the monopoly of the power of the rich, but man again does the same thing. All goes to the elder son.

Woman can create a just society with this money not one place but moving around, Indonesia, Malaysia, Turkey, Jordan, France, Greece and Rome.

There is no crime, nobody attacking you for anything all the men are happy because they know how to respect women from their mother. Everybody is happy when they have a daughter but not in North India and Pakistan. They are not following the Qur'an in India and now we are not afraid, seeing it through Qur'an. We are not only equal gender but superior gender. We have to take our position that the Qur'an gave us. Why we women should follow Rabiya a sufi saint. She and I feel total love for God. No fear at all. God loves us like a mother loves. We have seven heavens.

We are not afraid of bad monster political people. We follow Qur'an and love for God like Rabiya. We make it like heaven on earth men have to realise that your religion is in your heart. Man has to realise that Shariah Law is not Qur'an; it is made by the British people before they left India. Gandhi wanted freedom without killing Britishers but Muslims were fighting with them for 200 years, for self raj. But we are not fighting the British, we are fighting each other. We never fought under Mughul raj when we have 3000 years of history. Under the Mughul nobody fought against each other.

I want Prime Minister and all Indians to go back and learn the real history of Mughal and not British made history of Mughal. Muslims follow the British interpretation of Qur'an because they are afraid of their identity. The mean and jealous British are gone but we are still fighting each other. Women of India have to come as the woman of the world to realise this is not Qur'an. Everyday a little girl wants to go to school to want to help parents, men create all bad environments for them but the girls don't want to stay home anymore.

The essentially nineteenth century version of science has been rejected by many feminist social scientists. Science has recognised only one 'reality' and so only one valid view of it. The idea that reality is only one dimensional permits only one true description of its reality. In fact, different opinions, realities and facts exist in society. The nature of social facts, reality and participation in it looks different to a feminist. Being a feminist means different approaches for understanding and participating in social life. There are three crucial elements that exist in feminism. The first is the reality and acceptance that women are oppressed and don't deserve that type of treatment. The second concerns the insistence on the essential validity of experience of political and personal. The third belongs to feminist consciousness and the way they see reality 'differently'. Feminism argues that social structures can and must be understood through an exploration of relationships, experiences and interactions within the realm of social life.[20]

Women have dual vision of life because they can see as men see, since they have been brought up to search out and accommodate their view. But they also see it as women and as an oppressed group. For feminists, a third vision exists, "seeing differently" women have been used oppressively for their own good too long. Now women are mobilising all over the world to use their own power for their own purpose. Women should no longer permit their world to be run by men. As soon as women accomplish their superiority, they will create a superior and just world for all.[21]

There has been a positive transformation in women's empowerment and economical development. Although India still has to go a long way in attaining gender superiority and justice, its effort towards equality is more significant than its neighbouring country, Pakistan. It is easy not to gain superiority because preference for sons is as obvious as ever. In fact, it has increased recently, and the value of daughters is going down because of dowry and violence against girls. It is true that "women are tightly wedged between laws, sometimes in laws, and sometimes the legal laws, and if she resists, then she is branded and outlaw."[22]

Through new research women now knew they are superior to men. According to Sixth century, Qur'an gave Superiority of woman and now it should be a norm that women are superior.

We have to learn not to fight for men but to fight for women. This is our duty now to do gender jihad. Every woman on earth of course we have to fight with our superior brain and kind heart to take care of everybody. All the fake male superiority has been proven wrong now women are doing research work and they are not faking their research work. In every aspect of life, job and education, women are proven to be superior to men all the fake old myth are gone.

"The true business of civilisation has been in the hands of men is the lesson absorbed by every student of the traditional sources. How has this come to be? What process perpetrated these ideals may be the most important question for the self understanding and survival of the human species, to what extent was civilisation built on the bodies and services of women, unacknowledged, unpaid and unprotected in the main, is a subject apparently unfit for scholarly decency", said Adrienne Rich.[23]

Patriarchy means a system committed to the maintenance and reinforcement of male hegemony in all aspects of life, personal and private privilege and power to protect the distribution of power and privilege to those who are male.[24]

Women in Asia and Africa work 13 hours per week more than men, but are paid less per hour. Worldwide, women earn 30-40 per cent less than men for doing equal work. They are still treated as the objects or recipients of policy decisions rather than full participants in them. Worldwide, only ten percent of national legislature seats were held by women in 1987, and less than five per cent of the senior managers in the United National Legislature seats were held by women. The average women representation in Europe is 17 per cent, USA 13 per cent, Pakistan 17 per cent, and India 10.3 per cent even though the average is Asia is 15.2 per cent. Pakistan and India are considered part of Asia.[25]

The world accesses and reads male truths and male points of view, and don't forget the male defined objectivity. The experience of social science research is interesting and useful to examine because it reveals the existence of subtle forms of discrimination. Experience is often treated as somehow inferior to theoretically derived accounts of social phenomena. Discrimination, as defined, has three aspects. They are all interlinked: Overt discrimination means the enforcement of professional practices acknowledged as designed to guard and protect existing standards beliefs, procedures and productions. Covert discrimination include all assumptions made about 'right', 'correct', and 'valid' ways of thinking, behaving and writing. Self-discrimination cuts across both covert and overt discrimination because 'self' is a major source of gate keeping. One becomes part of existing and validated standard practices and knowledge.[26]

Through study and through data, it is clear that women need to learn about the real reason of the fall of women is not "God" but man. Women should have a society worthy for women. All states should adopt zero tolerance in favour of women. Women are not going to take it anymore.

Everybody participate in Gender Jihad. A peaceful happy world is ahead of us.

Bibliography

Chapter 1

1. *The Invisible Sex,* Adovasio pp. 62-110.

2. Jawaharlal Nehru, *The Discovey of India,* Oxford University Press, New Delhi, 1999, p. 50.

3. Sandhna Arya, *Women, Gender Equality and the State*, Deep and Deep Publications, New Delhi, pp. 62–72.

4. Jha, *Indian Women Today*, Volume 2, pp. 220–227.

5. Arunima Baruah, *Women in India: An Exhaustive Study*, Anmol Publications, New Delhi, 2003, pp. 103–104.

6. *Ibid.*

7. N. Upadhya and Rekha Pandey, *Women in India Past and Present*, Chugh Publication, Allahabad, 1990 pp. 182-189.

8. Jha, *Indian Women Today,* Vol. 2, pp. 220–223.

9. *M.A. Khan,* Women in Islam, Sublime Publication, Jaipur 2006, pp. 220-223.

10. *Ibid.*

11. Dr Kaukab Siddique, *The Struggle of Muslim Women*, American Society for Education and Religion, 1994, pp. 74–78.

12. A. Engineer, *The Right of Women in Islam*, New Dawn Press, U.S., 2004, pp. 12–16.

13. A. Engineer, *Rethinking Issues in Islam*, Orient Longman, Hyderabad, 1998, pp. 136-137.

14. *Ibid.*, pp. 136–137.

15. Joanna Liddle and Rama Joshi, *Daughters of Independence*, Zed Books Ltd., 1986, pp. 73, 136.

16. Premlata Pujari, *Indian Women Today*, Kanishka Publishers, New Delhi, 1996, p. 85.

17. L. Devasia, *Women in India*, Indian Social Institute, New Delhi, 1990, pp. 59-67.

18. Shahida Lateef, *Muslim Women in India*, Zed Book, New Jersey, 1990, pp. 128-130.

19. *Ibid.*, p. 150.

20. Philip Cohen, *India Emerging Power*, Brookig Institution Press, Washington 2001, pp. 28-29, 102–103.

21. Ashley Montagu, *The Natural Superiority of Women*, Macmillan Publishing Company, New York, p. 58.

22. Amina Wadud, *Quran and Women*, Oxford University Press, 1999, pp. 1, 2.

23. Gisella Webb, *Windows of Faith*, Syracuse University Press, New York, p. (xi)

Chapter 2

1. Ashley Montagu, *The Natural Superiority of Women*, Macmillan Publishing Company, New York, pp. 8–17.

2. Natalie Angier, *Woman – An Intimate Geography*, Anchor Books, USA, pp. 302, 303.

3. Natalie Angier, *Woman – An Intimate Geography*, Anchor Books, USA, pp. 306, 307.

4. William James, *Putting Evolutionary Psychology on the couch* (quoted by R.V. Short at the Conclusion of his book).

5. Jimmy Carter, *A Call to Action, Women, Religion, Violence and Power*, Simon and Schuster, New York, 2014, pp. 192-193.

6. Sudha Menon, *Legacy, Random House*, India, p. 255.

7. Jean Shinoda Bolen M.D., *Goddesses in Every Woman*, Harpar Collins, New York, p. xvii.

8. Ashley Montagu, *The Natural Superiority of Women*, Macmillan Publishing Company, New York, pp. 41–43.

9. Ashley Montagu, *The Natural Superiority of Women*, Macmillan Publishing Company, New York, pp. 70–81.

10. Jean Shinoda Bolen M.D., *Goddesses in Every Woman*, Harpar Collins, New York, p. 1.

11. Ashley Montagu, *The Natural Superiority of Women*, Macmillan Publishing Company, New York, pp. 88–89.

12. Asghar Ali Engineer, *Islam Gender Justice*, Gyan Publishing House, New Delhi, 2013, pp. 271-273.

13. Asghar Ali Engineer, *The Prophet of Non-Violence*, Vitasta Publishing House, New Delhi, p. 26, 27.

14. Louann Brisendine, M.D., *The Female Brain*, Crown Publishing, New York, pp. 14-16, 162,163.

15. Dan Abrams, *Man Down*, Liberty J. Group, 2011, (ebook).

16. Esther Waths, *Why the Best Man for the Job is a Woman*, Harper Collins, New York, 2007 (ebook).

17. Cordella Fine, *Delusion of Gender – The Real Science*, New York Company 2010 (ebook).

18. Sthor D. Myers, *Why Women should Rule the World*, Harper College, New York, 2008, (ebook).

19. Asghar Ali Engineer, *The Struggle of Muslim Women*, American Society for Education and Religion, USA, 1994, pp. 118-120.

20. Qamurdeen Khan, *Status of Women in Islam*, Bahwalpur, Pakistan, pp. 57–64.

21. Dr. Mahamd Ata, *The Hudud*, Alsid Sidahmad, Malasia, 1995, pp. 128–135.

22. *Ibid* pp.178-179.

23. Dr Kaukab Siddique, *The Struggle of Muslim Women*, American Society for Education and Religion, Bangladesh, 1993, pp. 90, 138, 139.

24. Ruth Blier, *Science and Gender*, Pergamon Press, New York, 1984, pp. 162-163.

25. Bill Clinton, *Giving*, Ransom House, New York, 2007, (ebook).

Chapter 3

1. B. N. Luniya, *Evolution of Indian Culture*, Lakshmi Narain Agarwal, 2005, pp. 42-43.

2. Uma Shankar Jha, *Indian Women Today*, Volume 2, Kanishka Publishers, New Delhi, 1996, p. 23.

3. Merlin Stone, *When God was a Woman*, Harvest/ Harcourt, USA.

4. Asghar Ali Engineer, *Islam Misgivings and History*, Vitasta Publishing Pvt. Limited, New Delhi, pp. 12, 13.

5. Asghar Ali Engineer, *The Prophet of Non-Violence*, Vitasta Publishing Pvt. Limited, New Delhi, pp. 5-7.

6. Asghar Ali Engineer, *Islam Restructuring Theology*, Vitasta Publishing Pvt. Limited, New Delhi, p. 54.

7. Jean Sasson, *Princess More Tears to Cry*.

8. *Ibid.*, pp. 80–5.

Chapter 4

1. Barbara Freyer Stowasser, *Women in the Quran*, Oxford University Press, New York, pp. 67-77.

2. B. Aisha Lemu/Fatima Heeren, *Woman and Islam*, Cromwell Press Ltd., Wiltshire, pp. 14-15.

3. B. Aisha Lemu/Fatima Heeren, *Woman and Islam*, Cromwell Press Ltd., Wiltshire, pp. 15-16.

4. Asghar Ali Engineer, *Islam Restructuring Theology*, Vitasta Publishing Pvt. Limited, New Delhi, pp. 24, 25.

5. Asghar Ali Engineer, *Islam Gender Justice*, Gyan Publishing House, New Delhi, 2013, p. 159.

6. Asghar Ali Engineer, *Rational Approach to Islam*, Gyan Publishing House, New Delhi, 2013, p. 25.

7. Dr Kaukab Siddique, *The Struggle of Muslim Women*, American Society for Education and Religion, Bangladesh,1993, p. 21-29.

8. Dr Kaukab Siddique, *The Struggle of Muslim Women*, American Society for Education and Religion, Bangladesh,1993, pp. 40-49.

9. Dr Kaukab Siddique, *The Struggle of Muslim Women*, American Society for Education and Religion, Bangladesh,1993, pp. 84-89.

10. Dr Kaukab Siddique, *The Struggle of Muslim Women*, American Society for Education and Religion, Bangladesh, 1993, pp. 93-94.

11. Asghar Ali Engineer, *Islam Misgivings and History*, Vitasta Publishing Pvt. Limited, New Delhi, pp. 135,136.

12. Asghar Ali Engineer, *The Prophet of Non-Violence*, Vitasta Publishing Pvt. Limited, New Delhi, p. 25.

13. Barbara Frayer Stowasser, *Women in the Quran*, Oxford University Press, New York, pp. 47, 48.

14. Dr Kaukab Siddique, *The Struggle of Muslim Women*, American Society for Education and Religion, Bangladesh, 1993, pp. 11, 12.

15. Amina Wadud, *Quran and Women*, Oxford University Press, 1999, p. 15.

16. Amina Wadud, *Quran and Women*, Oxford University Press, 1999, pp. 54-58.

17. Barbara Frayer Stowasser, *Women in the Quran*, Oxford University Press, New York, p. 49.

18. Barbara Frayer Stowasser, *Women in the Quran*, Oxford University Press, New York, pp. 63, 64.

19. Barbara Frayer Stowasser, *Women in the Quran*, Oxford University Press, New York, p. 68 .

20. Barbara Frayer Stowasser, *Women in the Quran*, Oxford University Press, New York, pp. 69, 71-81.

21. Barbara Frayer Stowasser, *Women in the Quran*, Oxford University Press, New York, pp. 109, 110.

22. Amina Wadud, *Quran and Women*, Oxford University Press, 1999, pp. 3-10.

23. Barbara Frayer Stowasser, *Women in the Quran*, Oxford University Press, New York, pp. 5-7.

24. Dr Kaukab Siddique, *The Struggle of Muslim Women*, American Society for Education and Religion, Bangladesh, 1993, pp. 40, 46, 47.

25. Dr Kaukab Siddique, *The Struggle of Muslim Women*, American Society for Education and Religion, Bangladesh, 1993, pp. 67, 71, 72.

Chapter 5

1. Asghar Ali Engineer, *Islam – Misgivings and History,* Vitasta Publishing House, New Delhi, pp. 130, 133, 179, 180.

2. Asghar Ali Engineer, *Islam Restructuring Theology*, Vitasta Publishing Pvt. Limited, New Delhi, pp. 13, 20.

3. Asghar Ali Engineer, *Islam Gender Justice*, Gyan Publishing House, New Delhi, 2013, pp. 33, 48.

4. Asghar Ali Engineer, *Islam Gender Justice*, Gyan Publishing House, New Delhi, 2013, pp. 51,56.

5. Asghar Ali Engineer, *Islam Gender Justice*, Gyan Publishing House, New Delhi, 2013, pp. 163,165.

6. Asghar Ali Engineer, *Islam Gender Justice*, Gyan Publishing House, New Delhi, 2013, pp. 166-169.

7. Asghar Ali Engineer, *Islam Gender Justice*, Gyan Publishing House, New Delhi, 2013, pp. 174, 175.

8. Dr Kaukab Siddique, *The Struggle of Muslim Women*, American Society for Education and Religion, Bangladesh, 1993, pp. 74, 75.

9. Dr Kaukab Siddique, *The Struggle of Muslim Women*, American Society for Education and Religion, Bangladesh, 1993, pp. 138-140.

10. Dr Kaukab Siddique, *The Struggle of Muslim Women*, American Society for Education and Religion, Bangladesh, 1993, pp. 136-140.

11. Asghar Ali Engineer, I*slam Misgivings and History*, Vitasta Publishing Pvt. Limited, New Delhi, pp. 136,137.

12. Asghar Ali Engineer, *Islam Misgivings and History*, Vitasta Publishing Pvt. Limited, New Delhi, pp. 180-182, 185.

13. Asghar Ali Engineer, *Islam Women and Gender Justice*, Gyan Publishing House, New Delhi, 2013, pp. 197-201.

14. Gisella Webb, *Windows of Faith*, Syracuse University Press, New York, pp. 5, 7, 8.

15. Gisella Webb, *Windows of Faith*, Syracuse University Press, New York, pp. 12-15.

16. Gisella Webb, *Windows of Faith*, Syracuse University Press, New York, pp. 16-18.

17. Riffat Hassan – *Human Rights in the Quranic Perspective*, Syracuse University Press, New York, pp. 241, 243.

18. Asghar Ali Engineer, *Islam Gender Justice*, Gyan Publishing House, New Delhi, 2013, p. 50.

19. Asghar Ali Engineer, *Islam Gender Justice*, Gyan Publishing House, New Delhi, 2013, pp. 82,83.

20. *Ibid.*

21. D. R. Kaarthikeyan, *Human Rights*, Gyan Publishing House, New Delhi, 2005, pp. 80-81.

22. *"Unreserved by a Man's World,"* The Times of India, New Delhi, May 11, 2003, p. 13.

23. Ruth Blier, *Science and Gender*, Pergamon Press, New York, 1984, pp. 162-163.

24. Maura O'Neil, *Women Speaking Women Listening*, Orbis Books, New York, 1990, pp. 54–55

25. B. N. Luniya, *Evolution of Indian Culture*, Lakshmi Narzain Agarwal, Agra, 2005, pp. 510–515.

26. A. Montagu, *The Natural Superiority of Women*, Coller Books, New York, pp. 235–340.

Index

A

Abbasid Rulers, 70
Abbasids, 69, 70
Abu Bakr, 94, 98, 113, 120
Acschylus, Greek Dramatist, 34
Adam, 80
Administration of Mosques, 133
Ahadith, 49, 128
AIDS Orphans, 63
Akbar, 71
Al Qaida, 71
Alaska Trail, 43
Al-Azhar University, 118
Ali Hussain Saibal, 73
All India
  Democratic Women
    Association, 144
  Muslim Personal Law, 145
  Secular Forum, 49
America's Puritan Traditions, 119
Amina Wadud, 114, 130, 148
  Saudi Women, 73
Anderson, Greta, Denmark, 42
Anglo-Mohammedan Law (AML), 127
Aristotle, 18, 52
Asiya, 84
Ata, Dr. Muhammad, 60
Atharveda, 66
Ayesha, 91, 93, 96, 112, 113, 132, 134, 138 see under Hazarat also

B

Bahadur Shah Zafar, 68
Bangladesh Military Academy, 132
Barelvis, Sunni by Sect, 120
Battle of Jamils, 100
Begum Syeda Abida Hussain, 55
Bengali
  Hindus, 73
  Muslims, 73
Bhatt, Ela, 38, 39
  Winner of Indira Gandhi for
    Peace, 39
Bhismapitamah, 67
Bhutto, Benazir, Pakistan PM, 33
Biblical Heritage, 107
Bishchoff, Prof, German Anatomist, 45
BJP, Hindu Communal Party, 141

British
  Imperialism, 73
  Law for Muslim Women, 69
  Slaves, 68

C

Cave of Hira, 71
Chadwick, Florence, US, 42
China, 63
Chromosomes, 46
Communal Violence, 49, 140
Constitutional
  Provisions, 17
  Rights, 22
Cultural Contamination, 118

D

Discrimination against Women, 57
District Kandhamal, 49
Divorce, 76

E

Economic
  Growth, 66
  Independence, 25
  Justice, 119
  Status, 25
Education, 15, 17, 19, 22-25, 32, 38, 62, 75, 76, 85, 120, 125, 142, 155
Egypt, 139
Engineer, Asghar Ali, 56
Equal Rights Amendment (ERA), 31
Eve, 80
Extremists, 69

F

Fatima, Muhammad Daughter, 112, 113
Fatwa (s), 94, 128, 131, 154
Female
  Brain, 50, 52, 53
  Image History, 106
Feminism, 126
Feminist Movement, 138, 139
Fiqh, 117
  Academy, 153
Fundamentalist, 119

G

Gabriel, 83, 102
Gandhi, Indira, 32
Gandhi, Mahatma, 68, 70, 72
Garden of Eden, 104
Gender
  Equality, 61
  Jihad, 20, 161
  Roles, 17
  Superiority for Women, 16
God-Male and Female, 122
Golda Meir, Israel PM, 32
Golden Age for Women, 52
Greek Knowledge and Philosophy, 69
Gulbadan Begum, Women Writer, 71

H

Hadith, 91, 94, 96-100, 120, 133, 134, 135, 137, 138, 144
Hafsa, Prophet's Wife, 60
Hajj
  Pilgrimage, 78
  Rules, 77

Hamida Banu Begum, Akbar's Mother, 71
Hanafii School, 98
Hasubai Buchari—Nisha Bulade, 49
Hazarat
  Abudllah, 95
  Ayesha, 61, 93, 94, 95, 100, 120, 121, 128
  Zainab, 88
Hijab, 77
Hill of
  Marwa, 102
  Safa, 102
Hindu
  And Muslim Countries, 68
  And Muslims, 72
  Code, 20
  Fanatics, 49
  Muslim Unity, 73
  Women, 68
Hindutva Agenda, 141
Hobbs, 18
Hudood
  Crimes, 60
  Laws, 60
Human Rights, 125
Humayun Nama, 68
Hussain, 88

I

Ijtihad, 117
India and Pakistan, 65, 69
Indian
  Muslim Women, 20
  Society, 17, 18
Infanticide, 115
Inheritance to Women, 115
Institute of Khalifa—, 88
Iraq, Syria, Egypt, 95
Islam, 20, 60, 70, 71, 84, 86, 88, 96, 116, 121, 131, 138, 144
  And Feminism, 99
  Treats Women as Slaves, 20
  Shariah, 142
Islamic
  Dress and Modesty, 133, 137
  Feminism, 126, 138
  Fundamentalist Movement, 139, 140
  Human Rights, 126
  Law, 118, 136, 141
  Movement, 134, 137
  Seminary to Deoband, 139
  Theology, 132
  Traditions, 129
Islamist Jurists, 49

J

Jahan Ara, 71
Jesus, 82, 83, 84, 112, 113
Jhang District Council, 55
Jihad, 55, 70, 79, 148
Jinnah and Nehru, 72
Jodha, Akbar's Wife, 71
Jordan, 139

K

Khadija, 71, 112
Kufah, 88

L

Lalch Baktiar, Women Scholar, 129
Landlord Women Community, 19
Legacy of Tafsir, 146

Locke, 18

M

Madina, 71, 95, 133, 143
Magna Carta, 149
Malala of Pakistan, 69
Male
  Dominated Society, 17
  Supermacist Cultures, 41
Maliki School, 98
Manu Smriti, 67
Mary, 109
  And Fatima, 112
Mother of Jesus, 82, 83
Mary's
  Chastity, 109
  Obedience, 111
  Virginity, 111
Masjid-e-Nabawi, 137
Materialistic Society, 21
Matriarchal
  Families, 18
  Tamil Nadu, Karnataka and Kerala, 18
  Society in India, 18
  Patriarchy, 115
Matrilocal
  Culture, 37
  System, 37
Maulvi Mumtaz Ali, 127
Mecca, 61, 71, 134, 135
Medicine Women, 54
Medieval Art, 70
Mehr, 86, 87
Militant Websites, 128
Modernity, 118
Moses, 84
Mumtaz Mahal, 71
Muslim
  Community, 24, 133, 134, 138, 140
  Countries, 139, 153
  Law, 127
  Personal Law (MPL), 127, 140, 141, 153
  Personal Law Board (MPLB), 128, 129, 142, 153
  Population, 132
  Religious Rights, 143
  Societies (ty), 22, 28, 126
  Women, 20-23, 28, 55, 68, 72, 130, 132, 133, 138, 139, 141, 142, 145, 146
  Women and Quran, 69
  Women in India, 19
  Women's Subsidies in America, 27
Myths, 30, 31

N

Naidu, Sarojini, 68
Nayars, 18
Neanderthats, 44
Nehru, Jawahar Lal, 16
Non-Governmental Organisations (NGOs), 142, 143
North Eastern Tribal Community, 19

O

Obama, (Barak), 15
Oppression of Women, Reasons for-, 139

P

Pakistan, 22, 139, 159
Pakistan's Women's Lawyers

Association, 55
Pandit, Vijaya Laxmi, 32
Paradise Lost, 80
Patriarchal
Judgment, 40
Society, 118
Personal Law, 141, 153
Board, 129
In India, 129
Plato, 52
Political Rights, 31
Polygamy, 20, 96, 115, 141, 152
Pre-Islamic Arab Culture, 70
Primordial water, 102
Prophet
Jesus, 109
John, 108
Zacharia, 108
Prophet's
Hadith, 130, 131
Wives, 113
Purdah, 20, 22, 23, 24

Q

Queen
Elizabeth I of England, 33
Jadwija, 33
Juliana, 33
Of Sheba, 107
Victoria, 33
Quran, 20-24, 26-28, 56-61, 70, 77-123, 126, 129, 130, 131, 134-136, 139, 147-161
And Hadith, 143
And Sunna, 116
Vs Hadith, 77
Quranic
Law, 20, 21
Teachings, 126

R

Racism, 30
Reformation, 119
Religious
Beliefs, 65
Identity, 21
Reproductive Cells, 46
Revolutionary Psychology, 37
Right To
Choose Marriage Patner, 20
Divorce, 139
Education, 139
Own Property, 139
Vote, 31
Rights of Orphans, 97
Role of Women in Karbala, 88, 89

S

Sahaba, 93, 95, 120
Salat, 99
Sara Mother of Isaac, 84
Saudi Arabia, 72, 73, 89, 139
Self Discrimination, 161
Self Employment Women's Association (SEWA), 39
Sex Cells, 47
Sexual Abuse of Slave Girls, 115
Shariah, 22, 56-60, 126, 128, 130
Law, 20, 21, 69, 126, 128, 141, 143
Sole Law of Islamic Faith, 20
School, 128
Shiah Muslims, 142
Sirimavo Bandaranaike, Sri Lankan PM, 32
Slavery, 69, 71, 156

Social
  Anarchy, 71
  And Religious Practices, 65
  Equality, 119
  Evils, 17
  Dowry, 17
  Female Infanticide, 17
  Sati, 17
  Justice, 28
  Patriarchy, 115
Status of Women, 67
System, 17
Socrates, 52
Solomon, 107
Sorcery and Witchcraft, 73
South Indian Societies, 18, 19
Spiritual Status of Women, 84
Status of Women, 66
  In India, 16
  In Islam, 146
Superiority of Women, 29-63
Supernatural, 30
Syeda Zainab, 88
System of Justice, 106

T

Tafsir, 27, 71, 103, 112, 135, 136
Teaching Women Surgery, 54
Textile Labour Association, 38
Thatcher, Margaret, UK PM, 33
Torah, 80
Torture and Murder, 15
Traditional
  Hindu Law, 141
  Indian Culture, 19
Tafsir, 27
Triple Divorce, 141

U

Umayyids, 69
UN Charter, 31
US Green Building Council, 62

V

Vedic and Pre-Vedic Period, 66

W

Wall of Zam Zam, 102
Wars of Islamic Expansion, 114
Weaker Sections, 77
Westernisation, 118
Women
  And Inheritance, 86-88
  In Asia and Africa, 160
  In Kuwait- Right to Vote, 139
  In Salat, 98
  Leaders, 19
  Of Power, 38
  Reservation in Jobs, 25
  Slavery, 150
  Superiority in Quran, 82
  Truck Drivers—Armed Services, 31
Women's
  Action Forum (WAF), 55, 56
  Biologists, 53
  Issues, 28
  Labour, 36
  Movements, 55
  Perspectives, 26
  Place in Society, 32
  Rights, 19, 66, 67, 77-123, 126, 127, 142
World
  Religions, 65-76
War I, 31

X

X Chromosomes, 47

Y

Y Chromosomes, 47
Yadav, Mulayam Singh, UP CM, 48
Yazid, 88
Young, Dick, 63

Z

Zamindari Abolition, 21
Zawj, 104, 105
Zihad, 115
Zimbabwe, 63